CONTENT

Introduction   3
The Internal Structure of a Modern Strip Planked Hull

Chapter 1
General Discussion About Strip Planking
1.1   General
1.2   Problems Associated with Strip Planking
1.3   What Hull Shapes can be Used?
1.4   Possible Changes to the Hull design   16

Chapter 2
The Building Jig   19
2.1   General   19
2.2   The Building Jig   20
2.3   The Strong Back   21
2.4   The Moulds   26
2.5   Mould Spacing   29
2.6   Setting Up the Moulds   30

Chapter 3
Internal Hull Structure   35
3.1   General   35
3.2   Internal Stem/Stern Post   36
3.3   Transom   38
3.4   Hog (Internal Keel)   39
3.5   Floors & Frames   41

Chapter 4
Materials for Strip Planking   45
4.1   The Planking   45
4.1.1   Square Edged   45
4.1.2   Cove/Convex (Bead and Cove)   46
4.1.3   Tongue and Groove (Speed Strip/Fast Strip)   47
4.2   The Species of Wood Used   48
4.3   Glues   49
4.4   Fastenings   51
4.5   Sheathing   52
4.6   Materials Quantities   53
4.6.1   Planking (incl. glue)   53
4.6.2   Glass Sheathing   56

Chapter 5
The Planking Process — **59**
5.1	Preparing the Jig	59
5.2	The Lay of the Planking (also refer to Chapter 1)	61
5.3	Joining the Plank Lengths	62
5.4	Planking	64

Chapter 6
Finishing the Hull — **69**
6.1	Cleaning Up the Hull	69
6.2	Glass Sheathing the Hull	70
6.3	Veneering the Hull	73
6.4	The Interior of the Hull	77
6.5	Internal Structure	78

Chapter 7
The Hull Exterior — **81**
7.1	Fitting Gunwales, Rubbers etc	81
7.2	Skeg, Deadwood and Wood Keels	82
7.2.1	Fitting Skegs/Deadwood	82
7.3	The Outer Stem	83
7.4	Bilge Runners	84

Chapter 8
Deck Superstructure — **85**
8.1	Decking	85
8.1.1	The Deck Structure	85
8.1.2	The Cockpit	89
8.1.3	The Deck	90
8.1.3.1	Sheathed Deck Covering	91
8.1.3.2	Teak Deck Covering	91
8.2	Coachhouses, Cabin Tops and Superstructures	92

Chapter 9
The Care & Repair of Strip Planked Hulls — **95**

INTRODUCTION

We have all admired beautiful round bilged boats sitting on the hard, newly painted and ready to kiss the sea, or sitting at their mooring with lovely rounded topsides glistening and reflected in the water. Surely, this is how yachts and small boats should be? - not with corners on! Well, you can argue that point for as long as you like. Personally, I feel that a clinker or multi chine design can look very much the part and there are very definite practical considerations that make multi chine or single chine boats, the most attractive form to have. I have also seen many round bilge boats which look hideously ugly perhaps because of a bad sheer line or too much tumblehome - or not enough!

But, there is no doubt about it, a well formed, carefully maintained round bilge hull has a beauty all it's own. The trouble is, whenever we think of round bilge yachts, we tend to automatically think of skilled boatbuilders carefully tapering long pieces of Mahogany or Teak so that they fit snugly without gaps against already carefully tapered and fitted planks. We think of skillfully caulking the seams between each plank - a magical art all by itself, knowing that if you get it wrong, the boat will leak like a sieve!

The well rounded strip planked hull of an Edwardian 26 by Richard Wiltshire.

Introduction

Strange then, that strip planking is not more prolific as a boat building method, at least not in Britain and, in many ways, strange that it has not been taken up with quite the vigour it might have been by boatbuilders in the 60's and 70's when traditional boatbuilding skills began to die, as the younger generation often decided against the low pay and long apprenticeship offered by the boatbuilding trade. However, right now some 50% of all commissioned new design here at Selway Fisher Design, is for strip planked boats of one kind or another.

First of all, let us look at exactly what strip planking is. As I have already implied, it is a method of construction which can be used to produce round bilged hulls without the need for traditional boatbuilding skills. In it's simplest form, it entails making a building jig which often consists of a series of fairly closely spaced chipboard moulds (sectional shapes of the hull) which are erected upside down onto a strong back (Figure 1). This building jig then becomes the form over which thin and narrow strips of wood are laid, each one being glued edge to edge with it's neighbour until the whole jig is covered, leaving you with a wood hull shell (Figure 2).

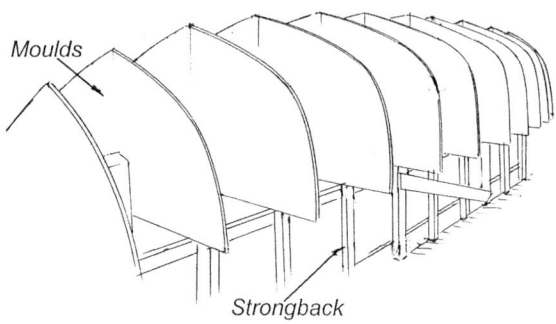

Fig 1. The building jig.

The thinness of the strips makes them easy to bend over the jig which allows them to be fitted without having to be steamed (as would be the case with conventional round bilged carvel planking) and the narrowness of the strips allows the majority of them to be put onto the jig without the need to taper them. In other words, they are kept rectangular in section throughout their length and the section is un-tapered.

Above—the building jig for an Indian Runner steam launch by Peter Stent.

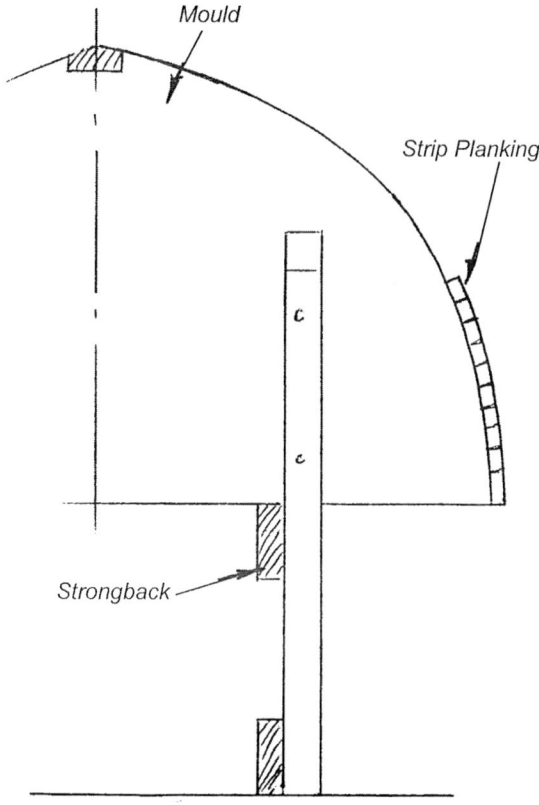

Fig 2. Planking over the jig.

Introduction

In early forms of strip planking and also occasionally today, the strips were not simply glued edge to edge, but also nailed through their edges to adjacent planks. This is possibly one reason why strip planking was not as popular as it might have been. Edge nailing takes time and a nail that follows it's own route and insists on poking out through the side of a plank can cause some irritation! If nails are put in at 4'' (100mm) intervals (Figure 3) and the boat is 30' (9m) long and there are 30 planks per side that means that there are............nails! If just 5% of those go skewiff (in my case more like 10-15%!) then you can appreciate, that that adds up to a lot of swear words!

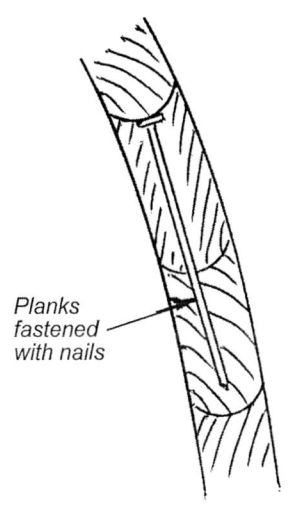

Fig 3. Edge nailing.

So why has strip planking come back into fashion? Well, the answer is largely due to modern glues and epoxies. The epoxies in particular, are able to provide a glue joint which is stronger than the wood that is being glued together, Consequently, there is no real need for nails to provide a mechanical fastening. If nails are used at all with epoxy, their main job is reduced to one of holding the planks in line with each other and making sure that the join between the planks is tight as the glue cures. But there are other ways of doing this without having to use nails.

The second reason for the increase in popularity of strip planking is that, obtaining the dry timber necessary for strip planking is easier with more timber merchants happy to supply relatively long lengths of thin strip timber. Some are able to supply the strips with convex/concave shaping to the edges, which, as we shall discuss later, can be an advantage.

A third reason, although not always of prime consideration to the amateur boatbuilder, but certainly to the designer, is the fine engineering properties that can be gained from using strip planking as a core material sandwiched by glass fabrics and epoxy or a hardwood veneer (Figure 4). This produces a true monocoque shell structure which, for it's weight, is much stronger and stiffer than the equivalent conventionally built carvel round bilge hull.

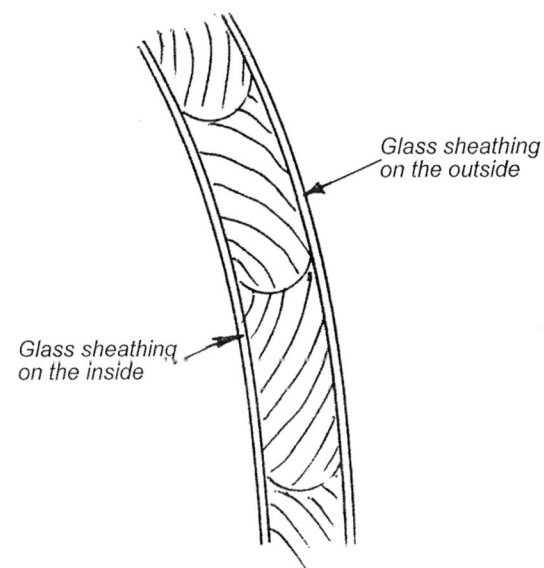

Fig 4. The Cedar core sheathed in glass/epoxy both sides.

Introduction

Above—the first planks being fitted over the jig on an Ijssel launch by Marc van Brummel.

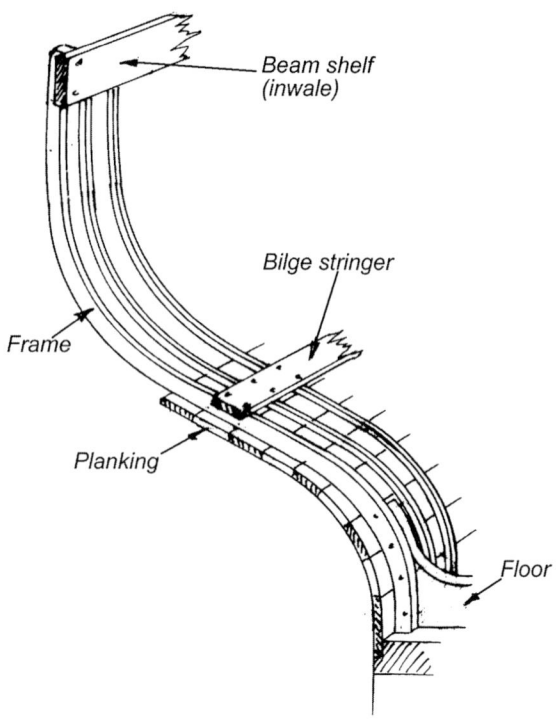

Fig 5a. A conventional framework for a carvel planked hull.

With a conventionally built carvel hull, which has individual planks fastened to a framework, the main strength of the structure comes from the framework itself. The framework will consist of a backbone (hog, stem and horn timber), frames and timbers, bilge stringer and beam clamp. The job of this framework is to be strong enough to take all the loads imposed upon it by the sea, motion, rigging, engine, rudder etc., and to be stiff enough to prevent changes in the shape and geometry of the boat. The carvel hull planking has the job of keeping the water out! - and this is simply hung onto the framework. In other words, on a conventionally built boat you end up with a stiff structural framework covered with pieces of wood which can in fact move. True, scantling rules do not forget that the longitudinal planks on a carvel boat do lend some strength and stiffness to the boat and therefore their contribution is to a certain extent, taken into account when calculating the scantlings (sizes) of the structural framework (Figure 5a).

A monocoque shell has it's own inherent stiffness and strength and therefore the framework can be much smaller and often comes down to simply taking the point loads imposed by rigging, keel, rudder etc and distributing them around the hull in a sensible manner – hence the aluminium internal space frames often seen in some racing yachts. A fibreglass hull is a good example of a monocoque shell structure with the exception that fibreglass does not produce good stiffness and strength at the same time. If a fibreglass hull was made so that it was simply able to withstand all the loads that it was subjected to, it would be too floppy. Approximately 30% more fibreglass has to be added to the hull in order to make it both strong and stiff. Hence the reason for foam sandwich hulls which have 2 thin skins of fibreglass separated by and attached to, a foam or balsa core giving both stiffness and strength at the same time.

Wood, for all the fact that it is about the oldest structural material used by man, is a wonderful engineering material. It has both strength (a piece of 2''x2'' pine on end can

Introduction

hold up 20 tons before crushing) and stiffness, at a low weight. So a hull of say, Cedar strips, glued edge to edge with a glue which is stronger than the wood itself produces a very stiff and strong shell structure. Sheath the hull on both sides, or even just on the outside, with a glass cloth in epoxy resin and you have a wear resistant, lightweight monocoque structure with constant geometric (it will not move) and mechanical properties - it will not absorb water and therefore it keeps its strength.

Going a step further, an even lighter weight inner core of lightweight Cedar planking can be used and then covered on the outside (or again both sides) with diagonal and fore and aft veneer of Mahogany. This produces a shell with strength fore and aft but also tremendous strength across the grain of the core wood - the diagonal veneers running at an angle to the inner core give excellent cross plank strength.

Cedar by itself, does not have good impact strength or resistance to surface indentation. Hence, combining a Cedar core with a harder outer veneer, whether it be glass cloth in epoxy resin or a hardwood veneer is essential in all but canoes and even then, it is highly advisable to sheath the outside with glass cloth.

Comparing the strip Cedar hull with a fibreglass sandwich hull, the foam or balsa core used in fibreglass sandwich construction only carries the shear forces imposed upon the hull skin and separates the 2 glass skins which carry all the bending and longitudinal loads. However, the Cedar core in a strip planked hull does take much of the longitudinal loading and the glass or wood veneer skins either side are only required to take some of the twisting and the transverse (side ways) loading. Therefore, the glass skins on a strip planked boat are much thinner than they are on a fibreglass sandwich boat.

As far as weight is concerned, it would be very difficult to engineer a strip planked Cedar/glass hull to be as light as a fibreglass sandwich hull, but the Cedar strip hull will be much tougher and more durable and in my book, much more pleasant to build. Compared with conventional carvel wood planked construction, a Cedar strip hull will certainly turn out lighter. A 30' (9.14m) traditional gaff cutter may have a plank thickness of 7/8'' (22mm) using hardwood carvel planks plus 1''x1'' (25x25mm) laminated frames at 8'' (200mm) centres, but the equivalent strip planked boat may use 5/8'' (15mm) Cedar strip with an outer diagonal layer of 4mm ply and 10 oz (350 gm) glass sheathing inside and out with virtually no framing. This will produce a one piece hull with no leakage problems through the shell. It will require less skill to build than a carvel constructed hull and the overall hull may be up to 25% lighter in weight. This reduction in weight will make the hull easier to move around in the building shed and will allow the builder to increase the amount of ballast, making her stiffer.

Working at McGruers on the Gareloch in the early 70's convinced me that working with thin pieces of wood glued together (laminated) was excellent practice. One reason is that you can more or less guarantee the quality of a piece of thin wood. Large bulks of timber may have all sorts of hidden sins inside them which are difficult to detect especially in a timber as large as a keel member. But this is also true of planking which may only be around 1 1/2'' (36mm) thick.

I can remember not long after joining

Introduction

McGruers we had been contracted to redesign and refit the accommodation and cabin top to "Josephine of Rhu", a beautiful 8 metre cruiser racer designed by James McGruer and built by A.H. Moody in 1952. Whilst we were doing this, the Lloyds surveyor gave her, her biannual survey and condemned a couple of planks. So we had those out and Liz our only female boatbuilder was given the job of making and fitting new planks.

Fitting the last plank is always the most difficult job, having to taper it carefully top and bottom to fit snugly against 2 adjacent planks and to arrange the scarfs on what ends up, as a plank which is over 30' long. The finished plank was around 5" (125mm) wide at it's centre tapered to 3 1/2" (90mm) at its ends with a scarf and around 1 1/2" (36mm) thick - a beautiful piece of solid Mahogany.

The day came to finally fasten the plank in place and I was on deck with the owner whilst we discussed his new cabin top. All of a sudden, there was the most filthy language you could imagine coming from below us. When we climbed down, Liz (who was normally a quiet soul) was doing a war dance and the plank, once glorious in it's full length, was looking decidedly sick with a great crack running across it's width half way down it's length. What Liz had not seen during all that time working on the plank was a thunder shake - a fracture in the fibre of the wood running across the plank - caused by bad felling or lightening strike and very often almost undetectable.

Working with thin veneers of wood or with thin planks for strip planking overcomes this problem because faults are immediately seen - the wood is too thin for faults to be hidden. The other side of the coin is that wood with minor faults can still be used because, being only a small part of the overall structure it's fault has less effect on the total structure. I have seen strip planked boats made from some pretty ropey materials - even from 2nd and 3rd grade Deal although I would not necessarily recommend it.

But to conclude this introduction, strip planking is an easy process to master, it can produce a beautiful boat as well as a very strong one. It has the benefit of requiring less internal structure which from the builders point of view, makes the boat quicker and cheaper to build. It produces a hull which requires less maintenance than a conventional planked hull. It does require the manufacture of a building jig which becomes redundant but this is often made from chipboard and low grade timber, so costs are not high. Also, some of the mould (sectional) shapes can be final bulkheads and with modern computer faired mould shapes, making the building jig is relatively easy.

It really does not need high wood working skills to produce a good hull. Patience is required as the process is inevitably slower than sheet ply construction but the reward is in the beauty of the finished product and those gleaming round topsides mirrored in the water!

Above—a 13' Woodlark Catboat fully planked, by Derek Hopkins—a good first project.

The Internal Structure of a Modern Strip Planked Hull

Different designs will have some or all of the above components. Some designs will not have any laminated frames and will rely only on plywood floors and frames/bulkheads for their athwartships (side to side) strength. Those that do have laminated frames will often have the inwales and bilge stringers mounted on the inboard faces of the laminated frames.

Hulls with counter or fantail sterns may have a separate horn timber (centreline member that connects the hog (inner wood keel) to the transom or counter frame or the hog may be continued right aft to the transom/counter frame.

Designs can often be altered to suit your own preferred internal structural arrangement depending on whether you want or need to sheath the inside of the hull planking.

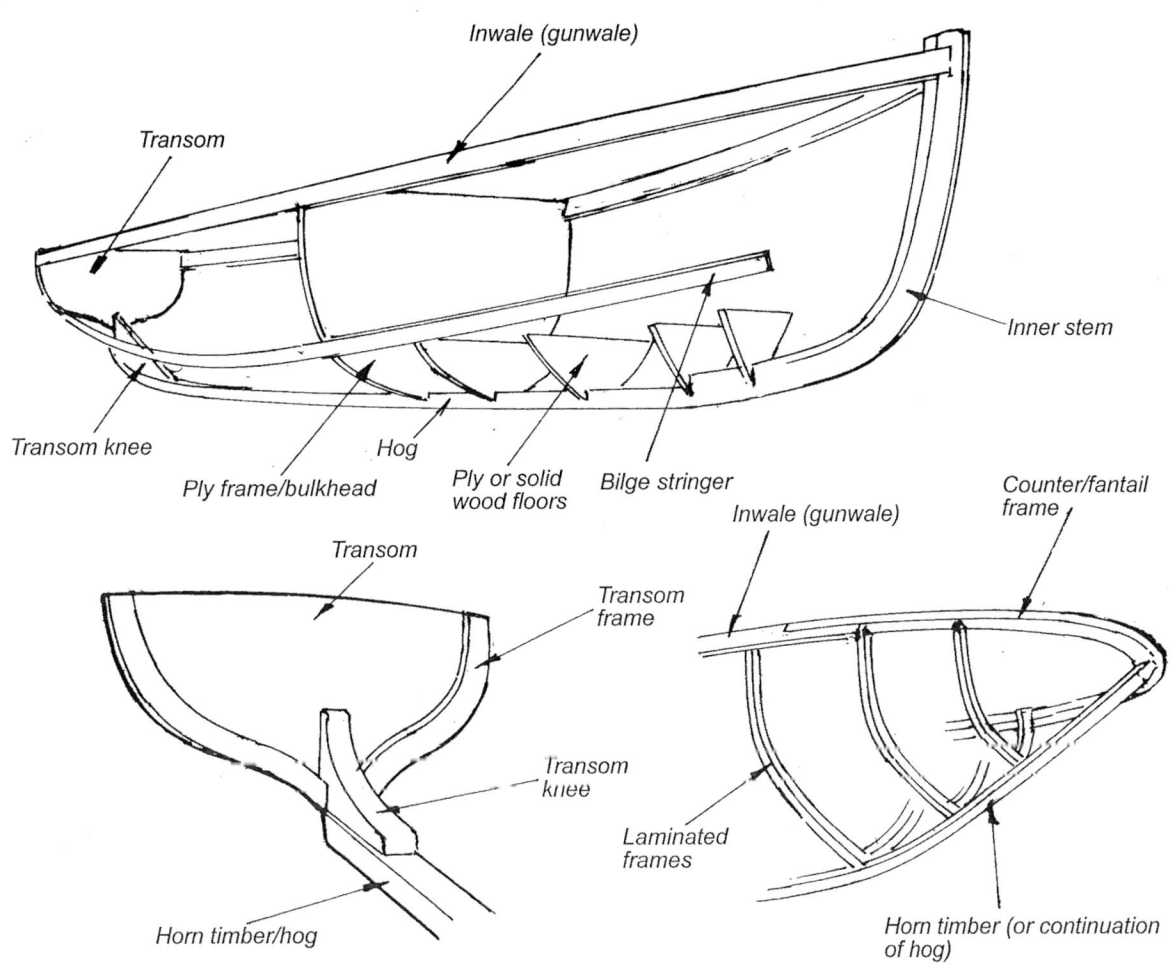

Fig 5b. The internal structure of a modern strip planked hull.

Introduction

There are several ways to tackle the construction of a strip planked hull—the picture left shows the moulds for Bob Kear's 25'6" Snow Bunting Steam Launch erected onto a strong back—note the cut-outs for the inwale, hog and bilge stringer—fitting the bilge stringer at this stage is easier than doing it when the hull is planked and turned over, but makes it difficult to sheath the inside of the hull.

Right—not only has the bilge stringer been fitted prior to planking on Wash Kohnke's 28'6" Corn Bunting steam launch but the engine and boiler beds have also been fitted—they are seen in this picture ready to be bevelled and trimmed before the planking goes on.

Go to page 18 for a picture of Bob Kear's Snow Bunting being planked—the picture left shows her planked and the outside diagonally veneered—the skeg/outer keel is seen in the fore ground ready to be finally fitted and bolted in place.

10

Chapter 1
GENERAL DISCUSSION
ABOUT STRIP PLANKING

1.1 General

Before we get into the actual construction of a strip planked hull and it's building jig, let us look at the type of hull which can be strip planked. We may, for instance, want to build a boat which has been designed for some other form of construction - clinker, carvel etc. What type of hull can be converted to strip planking and are there any limitations or changes that might need to be made?

The problem over this question, is that there are several variables which come into play. These include the thickness and width of the timber which is going to be used for the strip planked hull and linked to this, how much extra work are you, as the builder, prepared to put into the construction assuming that you can build virtually any type of hull so long as the strips are thin and narrow enough. If we take a particular hull, it may be a good idea to strip plank it with strips which are thick enough to give the required stiffness and strength to the hull without having to put additional veneers over the top to make it stiff and strong enough. On the other hand, some form of outside sheathing or veneering will be required if Cedar has been used for the strip planking, to protect the Cedar from abrasion and surface indentation. The thickness of strip plank chosen, will depend largely upon the complexity of the shape of the hull. Also, it would be useful to strip plank the hull with strips which are as wide as possible so that we can decrease the number of strips and thereby speed up the planking process.

If the hull has a complicated or awkward shape, we may have to end up using very narrow strips and perhaps multi layers of wood to faithfully reproduce the hull as originally designed.

Another consideration is the building jig. The thinner the strip planking, the closer spaced the moulds need to be. There is a mistake sometimes seen in strip planked hulls where the designer/ builder does not use enough moulds and consequently the planking is not well enough supported between the moulds. Also, it is often thought that there is no need to loft the hull or to use faired mould shapes because strip planking is 'self fairing'. These 2 problems are associated in that great care must be taken to make sure that the mould is absolutely correct and fair before strip planking starts and that there are an adequate number of moulds to support the planking as it goes on.

1.2 Problems Associated with Strip Planking

It is dangerous to assume that strips of wood will self align and automatically fair themselves especially if the spacing between the moulds is larger than it might be. Extra moulds erected in areas of high curvature (often at the ends of the boat) are usually worth the additional effort but even in areas where there is smaller amounts of curvature and where there are large areas of comparatively flat shape (ie. in the topsides), it is not safe to assume that the planking will simply 'self align'.

There can also be a tendency with hulls which are going to be strip planked and then veneered over, to spend less time on the strip planked part thinking that the veneering will cover any sins. In this case, whilst there is no need to spend so much time on the final finish of the strip planking, it is still essential that care is taken in the fairness of the strip planking - it's amazing how even 2 layers of 3mm diagonal veneer will still show unfairness in the strip planking below - beware! This problem with combined strip planked and veneered hulls is often compounded by forgetting that by using thinner strips of wood for the strip planking, these need to be supported by more closely spaced moulds on the building jig. There is nothing more ugly than a hull with the 'hungry dog' look caused by the strip planking taking the shortest route between the mould stations rather than being 'kind' to the builder and taking a gentle 'self fairing - great circle' route (Figure 6).

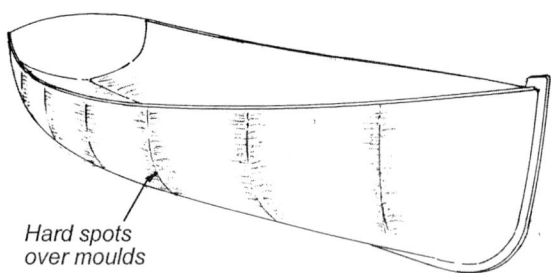

Fig 6. The 'hungry dog' look caused by too few moulds.

1.3 What Hull Shapes can be Used?

This comes down to how much time you are prepared to spend building the hull - the more complicated the shape, the more strips need to be used because the strips need to be narrower in order to bend into shape. Also, in the case of an un-veneered hull, how you want the planks to appear is important if the hull is to have a 'natural' finish.

Let us explain this last point in more detail. First of all, it must be appreciated that there is a problem, in that if we are using strips of wood which are not tapered towards their ends and which therefore do not take account of the fact that the girth at the ends of the boat is usually less than the girth at the middle of the boat. Therefore something peculiar has to happen to the way the strips lie on the hull for this geometric puzzle to work out. I say that the girth, which is the distance from gunwale to gunwale vertically around the hull of the boat, is usually, less at the ends of the boat because, with high speed power boats, the girth at the aft end is often the same as or slightly more that the girth amidships -(Figure 7).

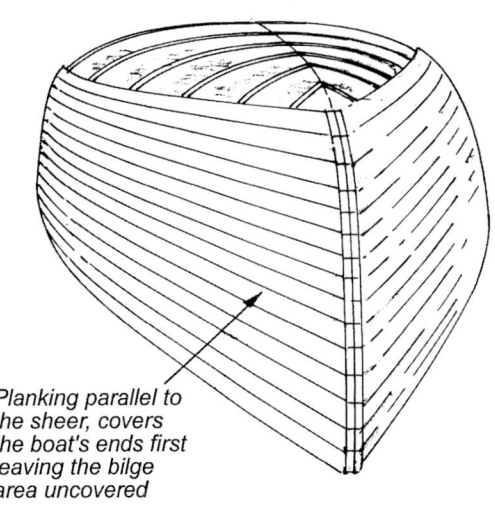

Fig 8. Starting the planking parallel to the shear line (gunwale).

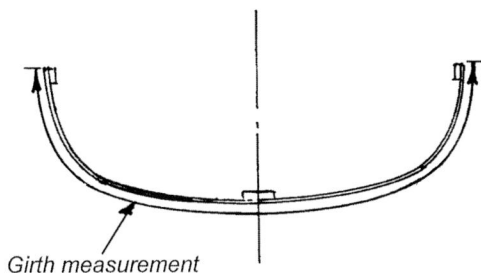

Fig 7. Measuring the 'girth' of the hull.

Now you can see why the planks in carvel and clinker construction taper as they go towards the ends of the boat. But what happens if all the planks, or in this case, strips, are parallel edged and un-tapered? Well, it depends where you start the planking process. If you start at the gunwale and plank towards the bottom of the boat, the planks initially follow the sheer line down to the bilge but then as you get towards the bottom of the boat, the ends of the boat become planked before the centre section. The bottom then requires short and usually highly curved planks to be fitted in the centre section, to make up the distance (Figure 8).

If you start from the bottom and work towards the gunwale, the effect is usually even more dramatic and by the time that you get to the topside the plank line has taken on a considerable sweeping curve up towards the ends leaving you with a section at the centre which needs to be filled with ever shortening lengths of plank. You can imagine that if you are going to finish the hull with varnish, this type of plank run is not very attractive (Figure 9).

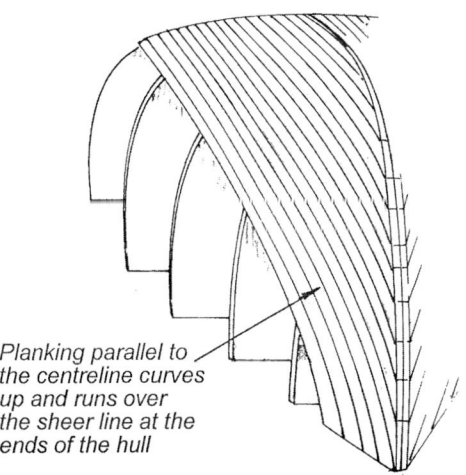

Fig 9. Starting the planking parallel to the centerline.

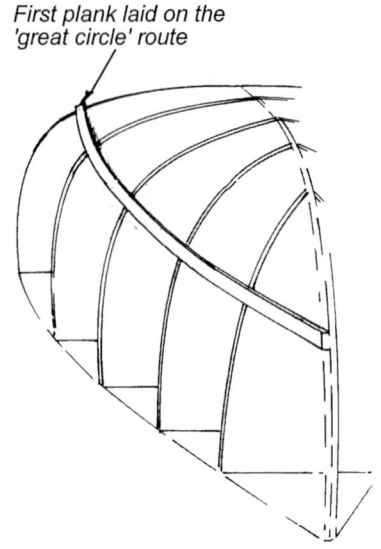

Fig 10. Starting the planking along the 'great circle' route.

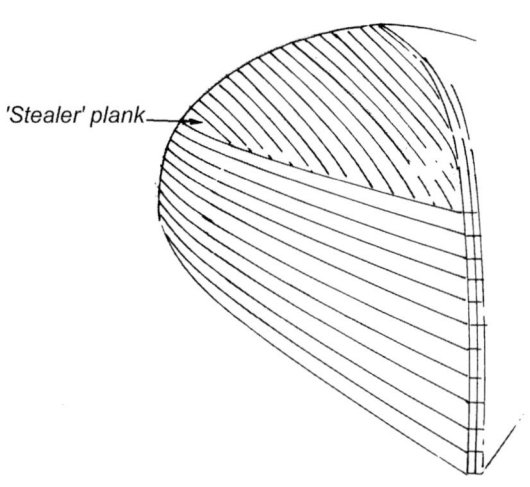

Fig 11. 'Stealer' planks used where planking meets, when it is applied from both the shear and centerline.

There are other alternatives. For instance, it is sometimes better to start by laying a plank along the 'great circle route' - roughly along the line of the bilge and plank either side of this. This method is often the best way to plank if the hull shape is awkward (Figure 10). Or you can plank from the gunwale and the bottom simultaneously and meet at the bilge at which point some tapered planks (sometimes called 'stealers') will be required to fill in the resulting oblong shape (Figure 11).

Depending on how wide the planks are, if you use the first method of planking and start at the gunwale, you may find that the edge-wise bend required of the planking as it goes below the bilge and approaches the bottom becomes too much for the plank to take. At this point you would need to use narrower planks or plank from the bottom up to meet the planking already done.

So, using the above individual methods of planking or a combination of them, there are virtually no hull shapes that could not be tackled with strip planking - it depends on how much aggravation you want.

The best hulls to strip plank are those with easy sweeping long curves to their shape with no large changes to beam and hull girth. Prominent fore foots are also sometimes a problem which means that hulls with a straight vertical stem and a deep forefoot are not always the easiest choice. Having said that though, by planking at an angle to the forefoot there is usually no problem but if the planking is run more or less at 90 degrees to the stem, the planking has to do a fair amount of twisting as it comes in from the wider sections of the hull (Figure 12). Laying some trial planks across the moulds will show this and indicate the best way to plank.

Double ended boats (those without a transom) are not always easy - especially canoe sterns. The fantail type of stern often seen on steam launches is the easiest stern to plank because the planks can simply run up the stern sections and run out over the back end of the hull (Figure 13).

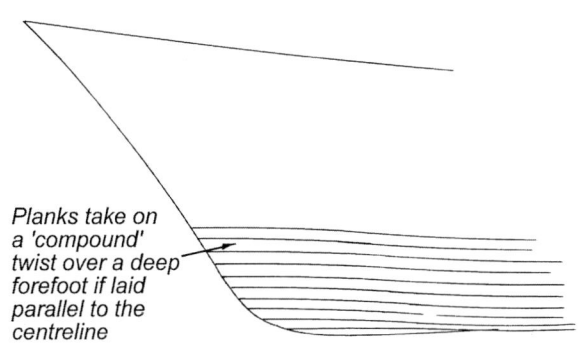

Fig 12. The planks take on a 'compound' twist when forced over the prominent forefoot of some designs.

Above—the deep forefoot of the Edwardian 26 showing the planks running up at an angle from the bilge allowing the plank to follow a natural curve without too much force.

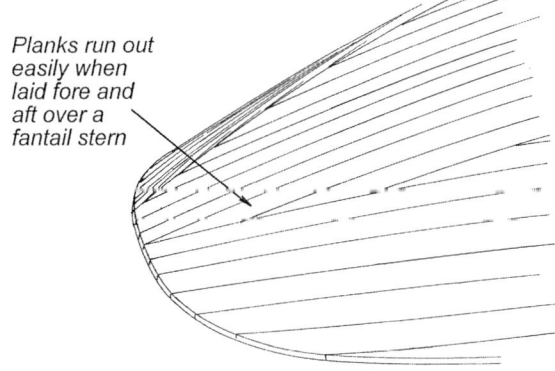

Fig 13. Rather than trying to force the planking around the sheer of a fantail stern, let it take the 'great circle' route and run out over the fantail.

Above—the stern of the Edwardian 26 showing the easy run of planks over the fantail stern.

Canoe sterns look deceptively easy to plank. They do in fact have a lot of 'quick' shape to them. In other words, their girth changes rapidly over a short distance. Certainly planking parallel to the sheer line can be almost impossible especially without steaming (Figure 14). It is far better with this shape of stern to start at the bilge and let the first planks take the 'great circle' route around the hull and then plank above and below this. This does mean that the planking will 'run out' over the gunwale with a sweeping curve. The trick here is to allow the first plank around the bilge to be laid as close to the horizontal as possible so that it is nearly parallel with the sheer line. The longer and thinner the boat, the easier this is to achieve.

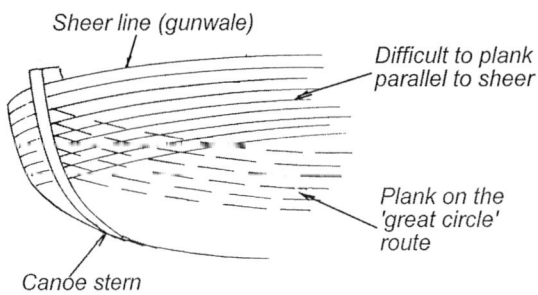

Fig 14. It is difficult, if not near impossible, to plank parallel to the shear line on a canoe sterned hull.

1.4 Possible Changes to the Hull Design

Hulls with hollow or reverse curve (concavity) in the garboards are also not easy to plank and it is often best, in conference with the designer to redesign this area of the hull to eliminate the curvature. Depending on the depth and severity of the curvature, removing it may alter the balance and volumetric displacement of the hull, consequently getting good advice is sensible (Figure 15).

If you insist on retaining the hollow garboards, you will certainly not be able to plank across them so this area will need to be planked along it's length first. This is good advice for any other problematic areas of the hull - always tackle the difficult areas first because the way in which they are planked will effect the planking on the remainder of the hull.

Think of how you are going to remove the hull from the building jig once the hull shell is complete. As with fibreglass hulls moulded in a female mould tool the hull cannot be extracted if there is any tumble-home to the topsides. If the hull does have tumblehome then you will not be able the lift the hull directly off the building jig which will be trapped inside (Figure 16). Again this may require redesigning the topsides so that the tumblehome is removed or the moulds will have to removed from the building jig in the region of the tumblehome before the hull is lifted from the jig. This may mean making the moulds split in two separable halves.

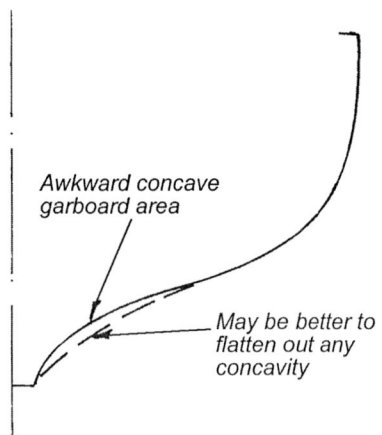

Fig 15. Removing concave curves on older designs to make them easier to strip plank.

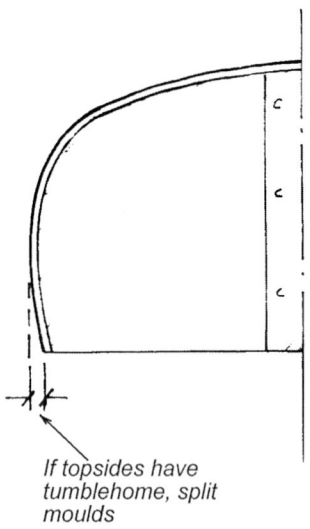

If topsides have tumblehome, split moulds

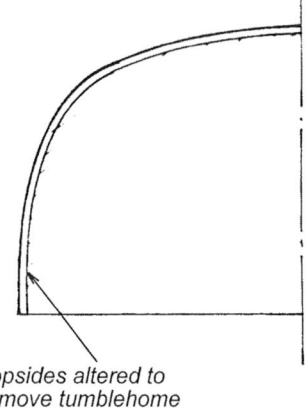

Topsides altered to remove tumblehome

Fig 16. Overcoming the difficulty of topsides with 'tumblehome'.

Talking of topsides, I personally do not like strip planking large flat areas or nearly flat areas. You may feel that nothing could be more simple than to plank a flat area. Not so I am afraid. Laying thin strips over an area which requires no bend from them means that any natural twist in the plank will show itself up. Bending a plank into a curve no matter how gentle, tends to make it 'behave' (unless you try to bend it too much). If a hull does have large flattish areas, then really strip planking is not the most advantageous method of construction. The problem comes when well rounded areas flow into flat areas. This is sometimes seen on motor yachts especially towards the bow (Figure 17). With some hulls a combination of sheet ply and strip planking is possible (we have done this on a proposed 60' motor yacht by having a strip planked round bilge area - with constant girth and ply 'V bottom and topsides) but this needs great care so that it does not look out of place. Otherwise there is no alternative but to strip plank the flat area, in which case do not be tempted to cut down on the number of mould stations used because there is no curvature - it is precisely in such low curvature or flat areas that closely spaced moulds are often required.

You would think that wide squat hulls with hard bilges and plumb stems with a deep forefoot are the hardest hulls to strip plank - typical of the North American Cat Boat in fact. Strangely, we have a couple of cat boats in our catalogue for strip planking and neither causes much problem in planking mainly because we have not used too hard a bilge allowing a more gentle transition from the topsides to the bottom.

If you are in any doubt about the suitability of a particular design for strip planking, then consult the designer first before going to the time and effort of making up the building jig.

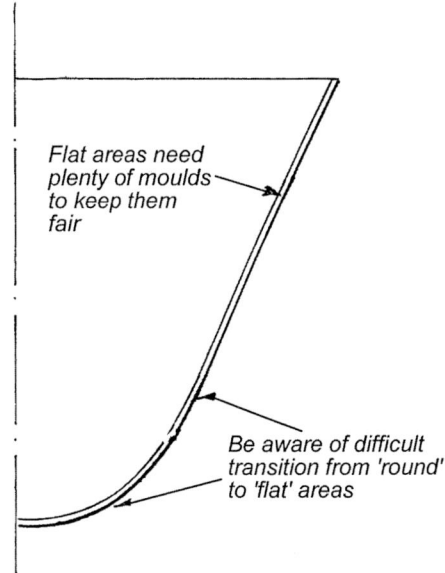

Fig 17. The additional requirements of a hull shape with flat topsides and tight bilge curves.

General advice can be had from Selway Fisher Design who can also offer computer fairing facilities allowing you to go straight into jig construction rather than having to loft the hull first.

Above—on wide hulls (hulls with a low length/ beam ratio) and especially have they have hard bilges, it is usually better to start the planking on the 'great circle' route as here on Derek Hopkins' 13' Woodlark catboat.

General Discussion

Left—the first Indian Runner built by Peter Stent showing the planking applied first from the sheer line and when then from the centreline with 'stealers' fitted (planks with tapered ends) between the two—this is often necessary on hull shapes with 'wineglass' shaped transoms and 'concavity' in the sections.

Right—long, narrow hulls like this 25'6" Snow Bunting built by Bob Kerr of Canada can often be planked from the sheer line in one go without the need to plank from the centreline—canoes can often be planked this way.

Left—another view of Richard Wiltshire's 26' Edwardian launch showing how, when starting the first plank on the 'great circle' route, the planks eventually run out over the sheer line (gunwale) in a banana shaped curve—this is fine if the hull is to be painted but does not appeal to everyone if the hull is to be varnished.

18

Chapter 2
THE BUILDING JIG

2.1 General

The building jig is the most important part of the whole process of strip planking. If it is incorrect in some way then the hull shell is going to be wrong. If the jig is out of true and has some form of twist or misalignment, then this problem will be duplicated in the hull itself. Consequently, whilst the building jig is, in essence, a simple tool and not very difficult to make from the point of view of necessary skills, it requires care and attention to detail in it's construction and whilst you may be impatient to get on with the planking of the hull, time spent making sure that the jig is perfect, is time well spent.

The jig is a temporary tool and in most cases you may only be taking one hull from it. Therefore, it does not need to be made from high grade materials. Almost certainly, once the hull has been removed you will want to break up the building jig as it will be taking up valuable space either in the workshop you are using or, over your partner's rose bed! The jig can be made to come apart easily and in fact, I like to build the jig so that it's main members can be used again for another job ie. a greenhouse. But, whilst it is together and doing it's job, it must be strong enough to retain it's shape and that of the hull shell without distortion and twist. On the other hand, the jig may be used by other builders who want the same hull and the jig may need to be made with transportation in mind.

The jig has to sustain being clambered upon and being moved, so it wants to be made out of substantial materials with strong fastenings. This does not in any way mean that expensive materials need to be used. Good strong Fir, Chipboard (or Sterling board) and stout steel coach bolts are all that are required and some of these can be obtained from reclamation yards as second hand materials. In fact, this is often a good way to obtain material, as timber in the form of old floor joists etc, which are still untwisted or unbowed can be guaranteed to remain true, rather than new timber which may still want to 'move' or warp.

2.2 The Building Jig

The building jig consists of two main components, namely the strong back which forms the base of the jig and the station moulds which are the sectional shapes for the hull (Figure 1 and 18). The moulds have a shape which is taken to the 'inside' of the planking, (ie., the outside shape of the moulds is the same as the inside shape of the hull planking) - Figure 32. The moulds have to be erected very carefully so that they are both 'square' to the strong back and at right angles to it. Great care has to be taken in order to ensure this and once erected, the moulds must be stiff enough to withstand any chance of them bending or buckling whilst the planking is being fitted.

The moulds are often bolted to the strongback so that their position can be altered if necessary and so that they can be removed easily should there be any problems in removing the hull from the jig. It is also prudent to use bulkheads as moulds thereby cutting out some work. How such bulkheads are used depends on how the hull shell is sheathed. If the inside of the hull is not going to be sheathed with glass cloth or with an inner veneer of hardwood then the planking can be fastened and glued directly to these bulkheads during the planking process. This can save a lot of time later and also means that the hull shell is well braced when it is turned over for fitting out.

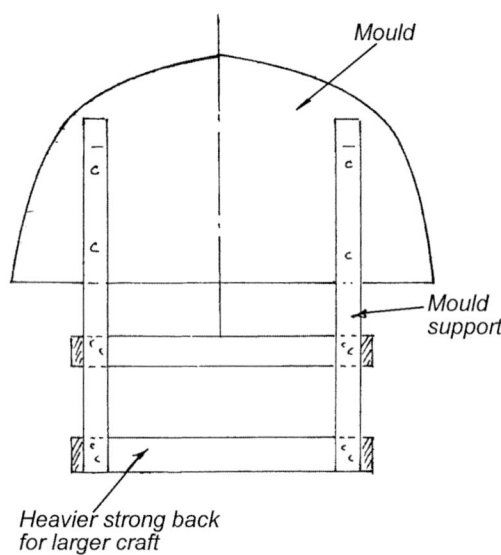

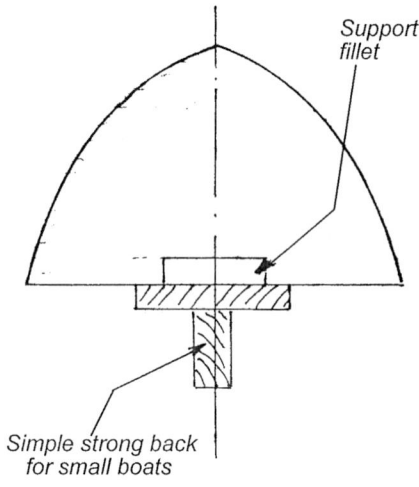

Fig 18. Typical strong back and moulds for a canoe (above) and a larger boat (below).

However, if the hull is to have some form of internal sheathing, then the bulkheads (which are acting as moulds) should not have the planking glued to them during the planking process. They can then be removed so that the internal sheathing can be applied easily when the hull has been turned upright. They are then refitted later over the sheathing.

The Building Jig

Above—the moulds set up with the laminated inner stem and hog (inner keel) on a simple rectangular frame strong back for a 17'9" Indian Runner built by Peter Stent.

The strong back can take several forms, as we shall discuss next. How it is built will depend very much upon the size of boat being built and whether more than one hull is to be built on the jig. The jig can be made to move for convenience by using casters, but these should be lockable. During the building process a fair amount of weight and pressure may be applied to the jig and therefore a good heavy stable strong back is desirable so that the whole structure does not move or tip over. For larger boats over 20' (6m) it's form should be widely spread so that it will not tip. However, it's size and shape must not interfere with the building of the hull.

2.3 The Strong Back

The strong back should have two main properties. First, it must be stiff so that it will not distort. For small boats and canoes, a plank on edge may do. But for larger dinghies and canoes, some form of box girder or 'U' channel shape becomes essential and for larger boats still, some form of substantial fabricated girder is necessary.

Second, it should be shaped so that it can give plenty of support to the moulds. This often means having a wide base so that the moulds can have more than one attachment point across their width (see later).

The materials used for the strong back and it's shape, will depend on the size of boat being built. As we have said, for canoes and small dinghies it may consist of a single beam running almost the full length of the boat. This beam can then be secured into vices on a long bench or cramped to a couple of stout work horses (Figure 19).

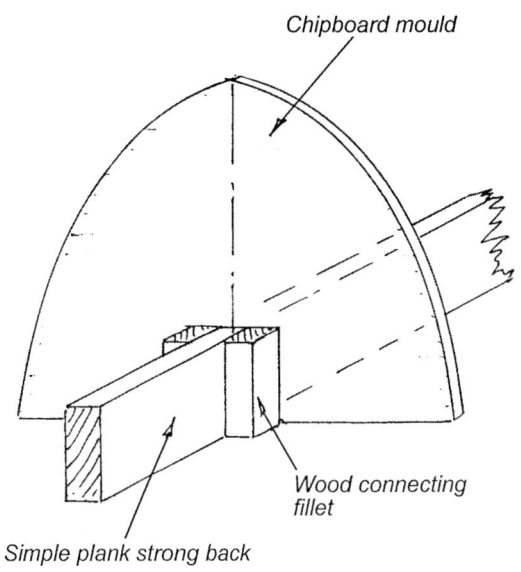

Fig 19. A simple plank strong back used to support the moulds for a strip planked canoe.

Better still, the beam can be a 'T' girder and made up from two pieces of 1 3/4"x 6" (45x150mm) or thicker timber (Figure 20). Good quality pine of some sort - kiln dried joinery pine or Deal is fine so long as it is straight and true without any twists or warps. I cannot emphasise this last point enough - do make sure that the timber is absolutely true. The 'T' girder shape is very stiff and gives more width to attach the moulds to.

The Building Jig

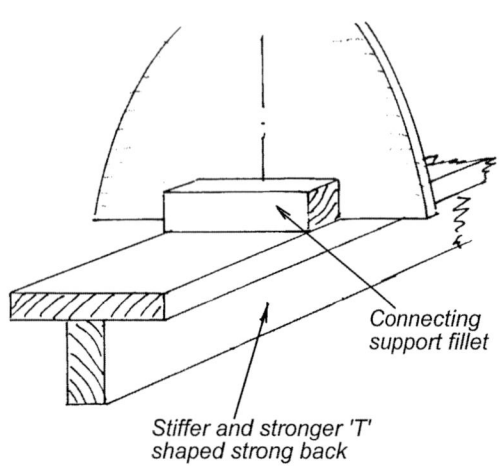

Fig 20. A 'T' shaped strong back.

The two pieces can be assembled into the 'T' shape by screwing the flat top piece to the top edge of the bottom piece with 3"x14g (75x14G) steel screws at 9" (225mm) staggered centres. Mark a centreline down the flat top piece and drill countersunk holes either side of the line for the screws.

Clamp the bottom piece to the top piece lining it up carefully with the centre of the flat top piece. Pilot drill for a few of the screws through the holes already drilled into the lower piece (Figure 21).

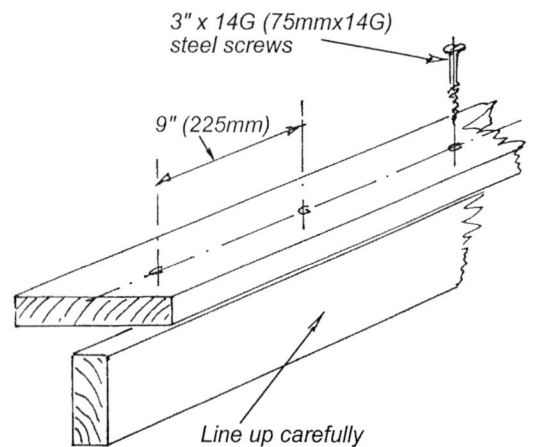

Fig 21. Assembling a 'T' shaped strong back.

Drive these screws and check that the two pieces are still in their correct position before fitting the remainder of the screws. There is no need to use glue. Both the plank on edge and 'T' girder type strong backs can be clamped in a couple of vices on a long bench top for support. However, you probably will not have a long bench available and in any case, clamping to a bench which may be against a wall does not allow easy access all round the hull. An alternative is to make up a simple support stand. For most canoes this stand has to be around 3' (915mm) high and wants to be substantial and large enough so that the hull/jig will not move when you are working on it (Figure 22). Most collapsable/portable work benches will not do unless they are used in pairs.

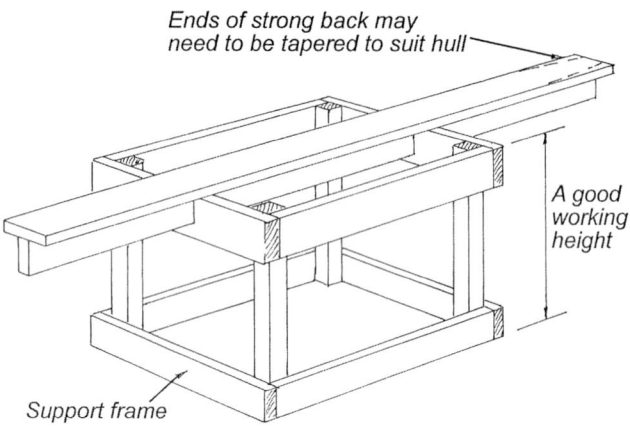

Fig 22. A simple support frame for the 'T' shaped strong back.

The plank on edge and 'T' girder are usually made from solid wood but if you would rather use plywood or even 'Stirling Board', a box girder or open girder shape is best. This can be made up using 1/2" or 3/4" (12mm or 18mm) material and for canoes and small dinghies it may be around 6" (150mm) wide and 6" deep (Figure 23). The easiest way to do this is to form an open trough with intermediate gussets inside the trough at roughly 2' (610mm) intervals along the length of the trough. The trough is set up with it's open side down and it is a good idea to make the top out of a double thickness of material to give you something substantial to screw into when mounting the moulds onto it.

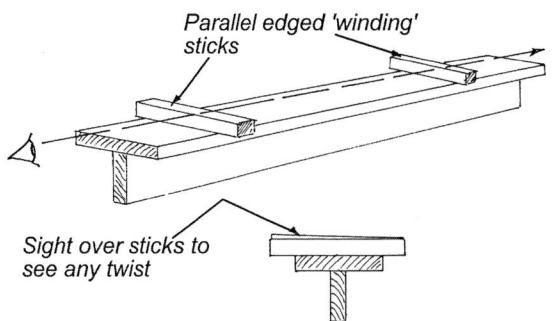

Fig 24. Using 'winding' sticks to check for twist.

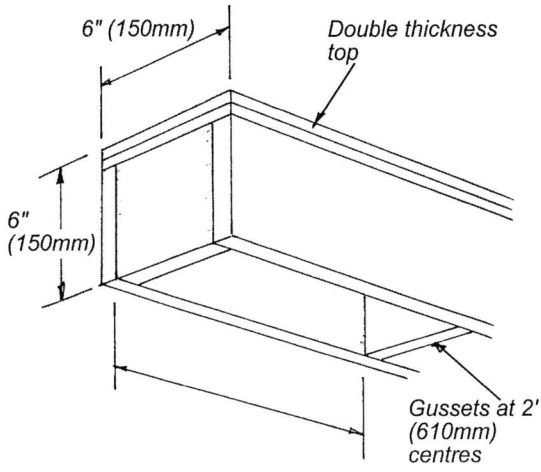

Fig 23. A simple 'box' type strong back.

If you do use plywood or 'Stirling Board', it is a good idea to paint it with some form of sealer so that it does not swell or warp in any way. During it's construction check constantly to make sure that it has no twist to it's top. You can use 'winding sticks' to do this. These are two parallel sides wood battens which are laid on top of the girder. By 'siting' over them you can see any warp or twist in the surface they are resting on. If the edges of the sticks are parallel to each other over the entire width then you know that there is no twist (Figure 24).

A small amount of twist can be planed out. This is easier to do on a 'T' girder where solid wood has been used, but whatever you do, make sure that the top surface of the strong back is perfectly flat. Any twist at this stage will duplicate itself into the hull.

The length of the girder will be dictated by the shape of the hull and the position of the moulds. Most hull forms have some sweep up to the sheer line at both ends of the boat and of course, at least at one end (unless the boat is a pram or scow shape) is going to be sharp. The strongback wants to give adequate support to the moulds at the ends of the boat and to any stem/stern former but not interfere with the hull planking. Hence, very often, the ends of the strong back are tapered. Also, the strongback itself is often shorter than the hull length so that the stem/stern overhangs and therefore, clears the ends of the strongback (Figure 25). If the drawings that you are working to do not give details for this, you

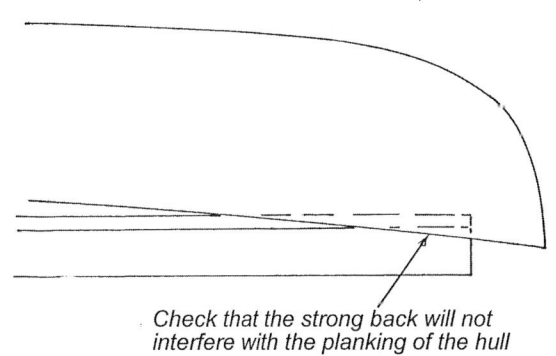

Fig 25. Taking the narrowing of the hull's beam into account when planning a strong back.

will have to work it out whilst you are making up the strongback. If you are not too sure, it is better to make it too long and to cut it down in length later. There is nothing worse, with a strong back, than not having sufficient length to support the ends of the hull properly.

For larger boats or for small heavy boats (steam launches and work boats) a box girder is not going to give you enough width to support the moulds on and so, some other form of strong back is needed. This usually takes the form of a fabricated girder. The timber that you use for this wants to be good straight grained lumber. A heavy pine is excellent and for boats around 18 to 20', 2"x4" (50x100) is fine. This can be made up as a rectangle with corner blocks and plywood gussets for strength and the whole structure can be bolted together with 9mm steel coach bolts (Figure 26).

Above—the rectangular strong back and mould supports set up ready to take the moulds on Derek Hopkins' 13' Woodlark Catboat.

give some stability to the hull as it is planked but if it is too wide, the uprights supporting the moulds will be so far out that they will not have sufficient length to be attached to the moulds properly (Figure 27).

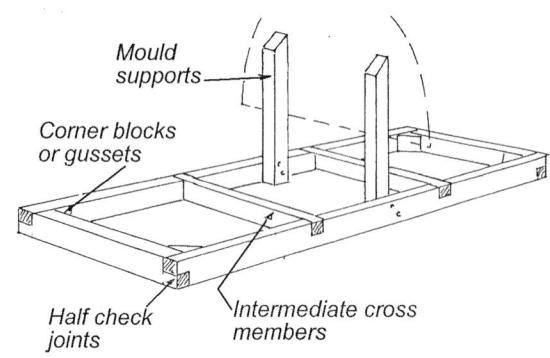

Fig 26. The girder often used as a strong back on larger craft.

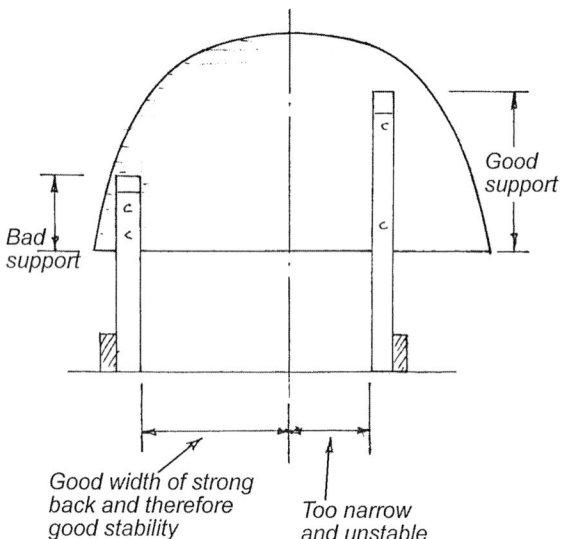

Fig 27. Planning the strong back and supports to give proper support to the moulds.

The rectangle can be subdivided by intermediate cross members half checked into the longitudinals to make it stiff. Again, the length and width will depend upon the hull shape. The moulds will be attached to the longitudinal members with uprights and this fact will determine the width of the rectangle. The width wants to be as wide as possible to

Obviously, if we allow the narrowest mould to dictate the width of the strongback, it will be far too narrow to be stable. Hence, at the ends, the rectangle is often sub-divided longitudinally so that the moulds at the bow and stern (if the hull is double ended) are well supported by uprights which are effectively held closer to the centreline of the boat (Figure 26).

This rectangular strongback can be put together using simple halving joints between the members but there are now, on the market, metal gussets and brackets which can be used to form the connections. Again, it is a matter of making sure that the strongback is square and that it's top surface is flat. However, to a certain extent this sort of fabricated girder assembly where the moulds are supported on uprights does allow you to erect the moulds without having to worry too much about the top surface of the strongback being totally flat and horizontal. Some adjustment to the moulds can be made to make sure that they are level by altering their vertical position on the support legs.

It is easier if you have the top of the strongback level so that you can use it as a reference simply by measuring vertically from it to a horizontal datum line on the moulds but the moulds should be checked to make sure that they are level by using a spirit level anyway. If the moulds are attached directly to the top of the strongback as in the case of the 'T' girder and box girder strong backs, the top surface really has to be flat.

For boats above 20' and up to 28' the strongback wants to be made up from 6"x2" (150x50) material. Also, the vertical supports for the moulds need to be braced with diagonal struts against the strongback (Figure 28). Above this length of boat and this form of strongback is not deep enough to provide the overall longitudinal stiffness required.

For boats above 28' two rectangular frameworks need to be made up and then separated by struts and diagonals to form a fabricated box girder assembly (Figure 29). In plan view this structure is not usually

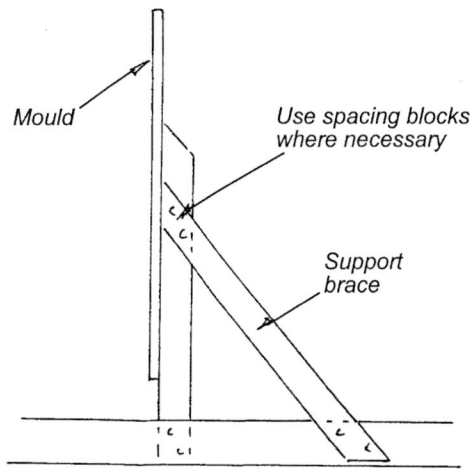

Fig 28. Diagonal bracing used to give additional stiffness to the mould supports.

rectangular in shape but diamond shaped. The reason for this is that, because such a structure tends to raise the hull above a comfortable working height, the hull is kept as low as possible by allowing it's ends to over hang the strongback as much as possible which usually means that the strongback needs to taper quite a lot.

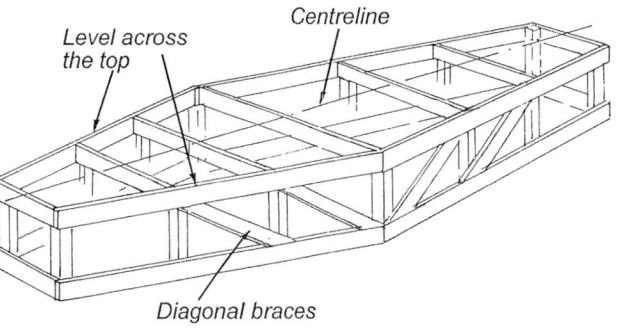

Fig 29. A fabricated box girder structure used for the strong back on larger craft.

Again, to keep the working height down, the moulds are very often attached directly to the strong back by their headstocks (see Figure 30) and this is easier if the top surface of the strongback is flat and untwisted.

There are no hard and fast rules for strong backs and you can adapt and change your own design to suit the hull and building area. In a boatyard where the building bay may often be a wood floor, there is sometimes no need for a strong back and the moulds are set up directly onto the building floor but this has the disadvantage that you cannot move the hull around.

2.4 The Moulds

The moulds form the shape of the boat and therefore need to be marked out accurately. They can be made up from any stiff and stable material. For smaller boats, 12mm or 18mm chipboard is often used. 'Stirling Board' may also be used although it's edges can be too flaky to get a good clean accurate edge on. Plywood is fine but rather expensive.

For larger boats, making them from a solid sheet of material can be wasteful and they will also be rather heavy. In this case, they are often made up from pieces of solid pine board or chipboard which are held together by gussets (Figure 30).

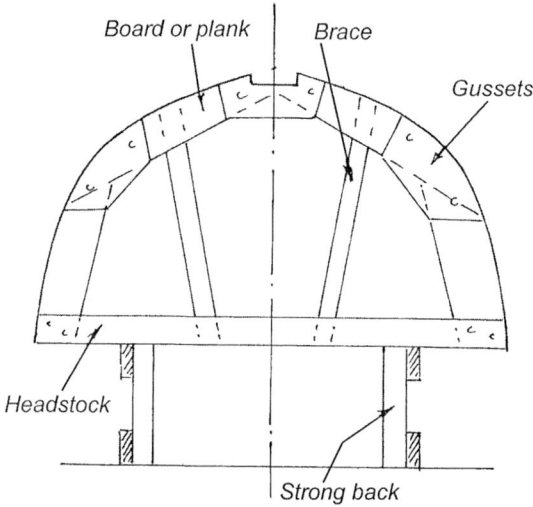

Fig 30. The moulds attached directly to the strong back using headstocks.

There are several ways of transferring the mould shapes onto the mould material. This will depend to a certain extent on how the designer has given you the information for the mould shapes. If you are working from a lines plan and offsets then the hull is going to have to be lofted full size in order to fair the lines and to obtain the mould shapes full size. (The lines plan of the boat is a drawing which basically shows a contour map of the hull with sections though the hull shape in each of the 3 planes. The offsets are the dimensions of the hull shape taken from reference lines to the hull planking). Lofting the hull is simply the process of taking the lines plan with it's offsets and drawing this down full size onto a floor (the loft floor). Immediately, you can see problems with doing this. First you need a floor large enough to draw the boat down onto. Second you need long accurate straight edges. Third you need long flexible battens - slightly longer than the length of the boat to draw in the curves. You also need patience and above all else, hard wearing knees!

Above—a combination of chipboard and thin plywood moulds used on Derek Hopkins' 13' Woodlark. The thin plywood moulds have had their edges thickened with scraps of chipboard.

But do not fret, with the permission of the designer, we can put the lines into our yacht computer system and fair the lines for you and produce the information that you need, without you having to loft the whole boat.

But why loft the boat? Why not just take the sectional shapes and their dimensions (offsets) and draw them down onto pieces of chipboard full size and then go straight into building the jig? Well first, the sectional shapes (otherwise known as the body plan) may not be positioned where you want to put the moulds on the jig. The spacing between the moulds depends upon the thickness of the strip planking and is usually less than the spacing between the sectional shapes on the average lines plan. So, drawing the lines down full size allows you to 'lift off' the intermediate shapes required for the moulds.

Second, no designer can read off the dimensions from a lines plan absolutely accurately using a scale rule. Hence the lines are drawn down full size so that any lumps and bumps can be 'ironed out' and do not become a permanent part of the actual hull. Yacht design software on the computer will do this for you and produce information for the mould shapes wherever you want to put them. So, if all the information you have is a lines plan and offsets, consider going to someone with the equipment to remove the need for full size lofting. If you are determined to loft there are several books which cover the subject.

What if the station shapes on the drawing are in the correct position for the moulds, can we just draw the shapes down full size and fair the hull just before we plank after the moulds have been erected onto the strong back? Very often there is some need to do a little fairing on the moulds before planking commences or at least to bevel the edges of the moulds so that the planking lies flat onto the edge of the mould. The fairing is done by taking one of the plank lengths and simple laying this over the moulds in various directions to see whether there are any high spots or hollows. Small adjustments are fine, but unless you are very fortunate, there might be quite a lot of fairing to do if the moulds have not been taken from a faired hull shape. In doing this, there is the danger of taking too much off a mould and having to take some off other moulds to re fair and there is no guarantee that you will remove the same amount from both sides of the hull.

Obviously, if the mould shapes are given by the designer as full size patterns then this saves a lot of time. But beware, if the patterns are on thin paper or on dye line printing paper, there is more than likely going to be inaccuracies which can cause problems. On a canoe type shape, small inaccuracies will not cause any real problems but on larger boats they can be significant. Dye line prints do stretch/shrink and distort quite badly because it is a semi wet printing process.

On larger craft, some designers have the facilities to give the builder the mould shapes on Mylar film. This is excellent but expensive and certainly not cost effective on any boat less than 30'.

More and more people now have access to computer controlled drafting and drawing facilities and in this case we, along with some other designers can give the mould shapes on computer disc in DXF format.

The way that we and some other designers present the information for the mould shapes is in the form of scale drawings of the moulds which are divided up into equally spaced horizontal lines (waterlines). The full size dimensions are given along each of these waterlines from the centreline of the boat to the curve of the hull. The dimensions are taken from a computer model of the hull which has been faired on the computer – therefore the full-size dimensions given are accurate and there is no need for the builder to draw the entire lines plan full-size and 'loft' the mould shapes from the lines. The shape for each mould is simply drawn full size directly onto the chipboard from the measurements given. We have found this to be a very accurate way to gain the mould shapes and it does not take very much time to do it. We have had boats from 13' to 50' built using this method and in each case the comment has been that the moulds have gone up and not needed any fairing whatsoever (Figure 31).

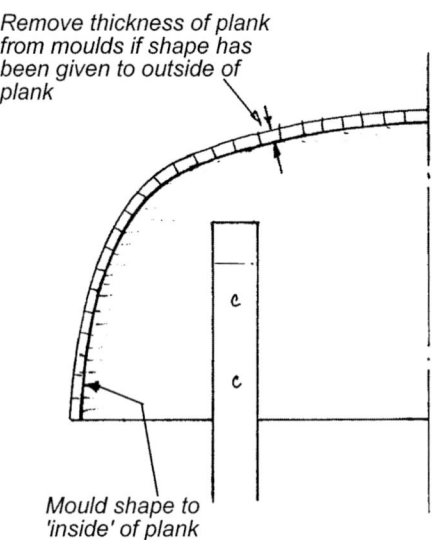

Fig 32. If the mould shapes are given to 'outside' of plank, the plank thickness needs to be removed from the moulds.

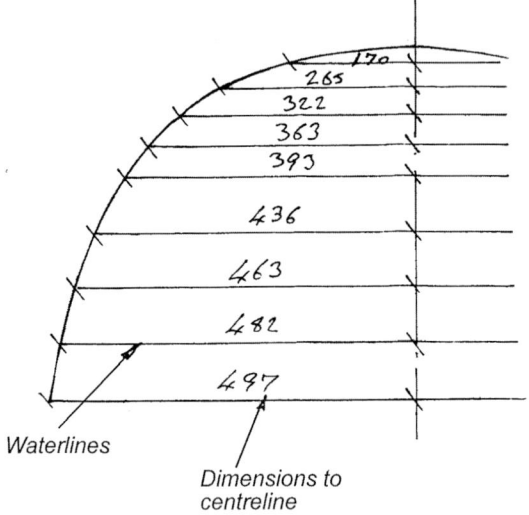

Fig 31. Defining the mould shapes by a series of computer generated dimensions along waterlines.

Whatever form the mould shapes are given in, you need them drawn to the 'inside' of the planking. If you are working from a lines plan, then the lines may have been drawn to the 'outside' of the planking. You must check this and if drawn to the outside, you will need to take off an allowance for the planking thickness from the mould shapes (Figure 32).

If the shapes for the moulds have been given as paper patterns then only one half of the mould will usually be shown and each mould shape may be drawn one on top of the other on a common centreline. In this case draw a centreline onto the mould material and fold the pattern accurately along the marked centreline and offer this up carefully to the centreline that you have drawn down. The shape can then be 'pricked' through the paper with the point of a compass and a flexible batten (or for small mould shapes, a 'flexi-curve') used to connect the points up (Figure 33).

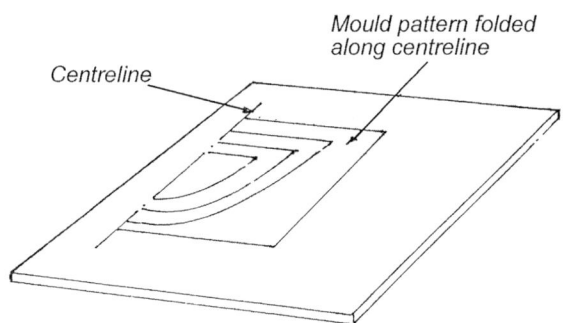

Fig 33. Drawing the mould shapes down from full-size paper patterns.

The old 'primary school' method of scribbling with a soft pencil on the reverse side of the pattern paper over where the pattern line is and then putting the paper down right way up and tracing along the mould line so that the soft pencil scribbling leaves a mark on the mould material, will also work. Or use carbon paper for the same effect.

If the patterns are drawn down separately then they may be cut out and drawn round. But whatever method you use, make sure that the paper lies flat and that you match up the centreline and any other reference lines carefully.

If you are working from a lines plan and lofting, then the end result is very often, the mould shapes drawn down one on top of the other with common centreline and waterlines on a piece of chipboard. The 'old' way of transferring these shapes is the 'half nail' method. You simply take some nails with large heads (clout nails) and file or cut off half the head. These nails are then laid down closely spaced with their heads on the mould shape line. The mould material is then carefully laid down over the nails without disturbing them. Pressure is then applied (you stand on the mould material) and hey presto the half of the nail heads which are left standing up impress themselves into the underside of the mould material. It sounds crude, but it does work (Figure 34).

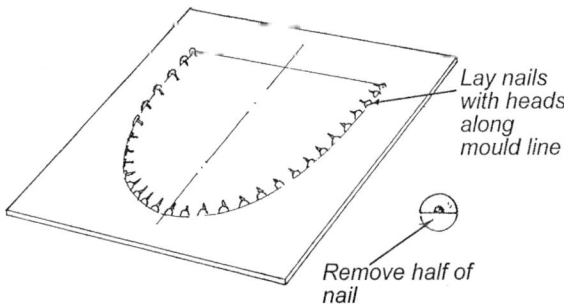

Fig 34. The 'half nail' method of transferring the mould shapes from a lofted body plan.

Once marked out, the mould shapes want to be very carefully cut out and planed accurately to the line. Take your time over this and run your eye along the edges of the moulds to make sure that there is no unfairness.

2.5 Mould Spacing

The spacing between the moulds is dictated by two factors. The first factor is the thickness of the planking stock. The moulds need to be spaced so that they give adequate support to the planking in such a way that the planking runs in a fair curve from one end of the boat to the other. Moulds which are spaced too far apart will allow the planking to go the 'least distance' route and the planking will be unfair and have the 'hungry dog' look (Figure 6).

Second, the distance between the moulds will depend upon the complexity of the hull shape. Both large flat areas and areas of 'tight' curvature will need extra support. Very often and especially towards the ends of the boat, it is necessary to put in intermediate extra moulds. For instance, if the moulds are spaced at 600mm intervals over most of the hull then there may be some at the bow and stern spaced at 300mm to give additional support where there is often more 'curve' in the hull.

The general guide line for mould spacing is quite simple. The thinner the planking, the closer the moulds. So, for a canoe using just 5 or 6mm thick planking stock, but with a long thin hull shape with little tight curvature in it, the spacing might be 18" (450mm). However, a dinghy shape of say 12' to 16' length (3.66m to 4.88m) again using 6mm planking, may have it's moulds spaced at 12" (305mm) centres, because it has more 'shape' at it's ends, (ie. a wineglass transom and a hard bilged mid section running into a deep forefoot at the bow).

For dayboat and motor boat hull forms where 1/2" (12mm) planking is used the distance between moulds may be 16" (400mm). 3/4" (18mm) planking may have 20" (500mm) spacing and 1" (25mm) planking would have perhaps 30" (760mm) between the moulds. These are average figures based upon the use of Cedar for the planking. Stiffer woods will require fewer moulds for support. For 5/8" (15mm) planking which is quite popular for smaller yachts (when used with glass sheathing or veneers) the spacing would average out at 18" (450mm).

Do be careful when using these figures and if the particular wood that you are using for the planking seems to be running unfair between the moulds, provide more moulds to support it. Also remember that these distances are for the Cedar strip planking only and not for the overall plank thickness. For a hull with 1/2" (12mm) Cedar strip planking covered by a couple of 1.5mm Mahogany diagonal veneers on the outside to a total thickness of 15mm, do not use a mould spacing for 15mm planking (ie. 18"/450mm). If you do, you may end up with the 'hungry dog' look. The moulds should be set up for 12mm planking (ie. 16"/400mm).

2.6 Setting Up the Moulds

Having spent much time and effort in setting up an accurate strong back and shaping an accurate set of moulds, it is important that the two are fastened together carefully. First of all, the moulds should have at least two reference lines marked on each of them. They are the centreline and a horizontal datum line. This datum line may simply be the top of each mould (or headstock) or a waterline. In any case, both reference lines will be at 90 degrees to each other and they should be drawn on to each mould carefully (Figure 35).

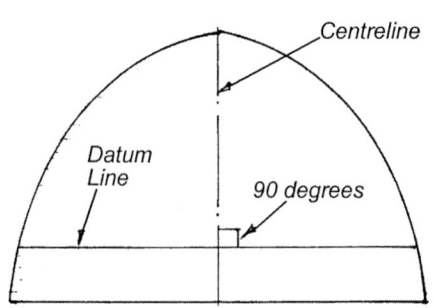

Fig 35. The reference lines on the moulds.

Secondly, the strong back should have two sets of reference lines marked on to it too. The first, like that on the moulds, is the centreline. This may be a taut line of string stretched from one end of the strong back to the other or, for plank and box girder type strong backs an actual line drawn onto the top surface of the strong back. The easiest way to do this is to hammer a nail into each end and to stretch a string between the nails so that it lies on top of the strongback. Use a spray can of black paint and spray over the string. When this has dried, remove the string and you should be left with an accurate straight line on the top surface where the string has prevented the paint from going onto the strong back. The moulds will of course be erected so that the centrelines marked on them are all directly over the centreline marked onto the strong back.

The second set of reference lines marked onto the strong back, are the lines which mark the position of each mould. These lines will go across the top surface of the strong back and must be marked with great care to position the moulds accurately along the strong back. It is essential that these lines are at 90 degrees to the centreline. How they are marked will depend upon the type of strong back you have made. For a small plank or box girder type strong back you can use a set square to mark them, after you have established their fore and aft position.

Looking at the drawing of the building jig set up you will see which side of the mould position line the moulds are to be fastened too. Usually moulds forward of the midships position are fastened onto the strong back with their aft faces on the mould position lines and moulds aft of the midships position are fastened with their forward faces on the mould position lines. This is done so that the moulds will have their edges bevelled to allow the planks to lie flat against them. If the forward moulds were positioned with their forward faces (sides) on the mould position lines, only the forward top corner of the moulds would touch the planking. This may make fastening the planking to the moulds difficult and may also, on thinner planking, lead to hard spots on the planking because of the lack of 'contact area' between the planking and the moulds (Figure 36).

To mark the mould positions onto the strong back it is best to start from the centre mould position and work towards the bow and stern. For the centre mould, set up the position line across the strong back perpendicular to the centreline either with a square, on small strong backs, or possibly by using the arc method. This simply means using a compass (a pencil on a length of string) with it's centre at the intersection of the mould position and the centreline to tick off two points equidistant from the intersection (Figure 37). Move the centre of your compass to these points and swing in two arcs, one on either side of the centreline at each point. Where

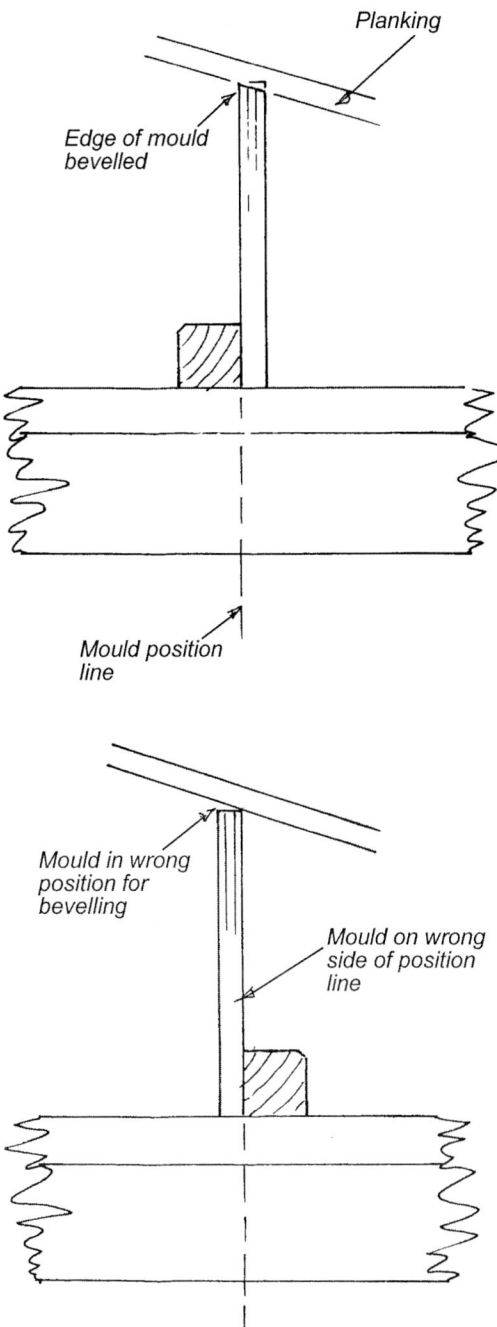

Fig 36. Positioning the moulds along the strong back.

these arcs cross will be exactly perpendicular to the intersection between the centerline and the mould position line and drawing a line through all three points will give you a line in the correct position and at 90 degrees to the

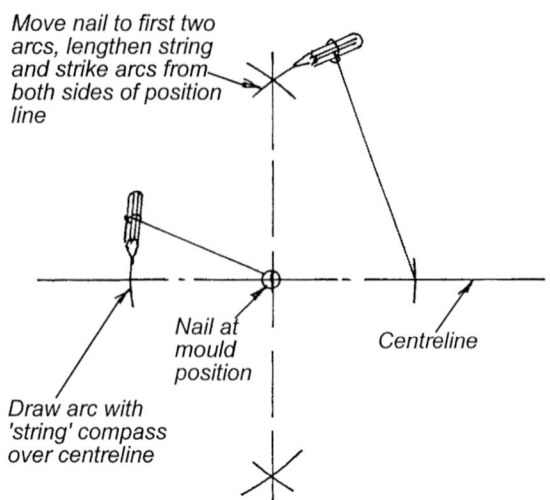

Fig 37. Setting out the mould position across the strong back.

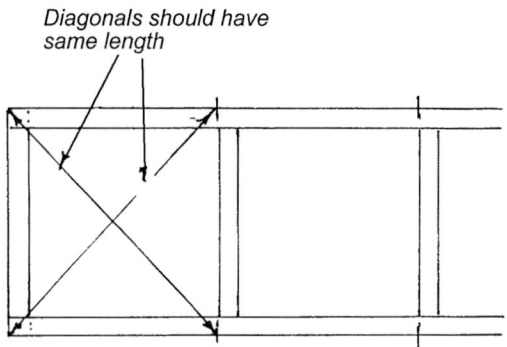

Fig 38. Checking that the moulds are positioned 'square' across the strong back.

centreline. This is obviously easiest to do if you are using a building floor rather than a strongback and have a flat surface to work on.

For a rectangular strong back, mark the position lines on one side of the strong back (longitudinal) and erect perpendiculars to these points, across the strongback to the other side of the strong back. A variation of the arc method will do this for you. Again use the compass with it's centre on the position mark to swing in two points equidistant from the position mark. Move the centre of your string compass to these two points and swing in arcs on the opposite side of the strong back. Where they intersect will give you a point on the opposite side which is perpendicular to the original mould position.

At all times check for accuracy. Measure the diagonals between adjacent mould position points to make sure that your marks are all 'square' to each other (Figure 38).

Once you have marked the mould positions, use arrows to mark which side of the position line the moulds are to go. In actually erecting the moulds, three points have to be considered and checked. First, that they are in the correct position (accurate marking of the position lines and erecting the moulds on the correct side of the line will achieve this). Second, that they are perpendicular in all three planes. They must be checked across the strong back, in the vertical plane and in plan view. Third, the method of fixing the moulds in position must be stiff enough to take the planking process. Cross braces may have to be used to achieve the necessary support.

The moulds may be attached to the strongback directly by simple wood fillets or by the headstock of the mould, or on legs. In the latter case, it is often better to attach the legs to the strong back first and to attach the mould to the legs afterwards. The use of carriage bolts is preferred because it is easier to slack them off in order to use 'shims' between the various components to make final adjustments and to get everything square and level.

If the moulds are being attached directly to the strong back using wood fillets, screw/bolt the fillets to the strong back first. Carefully clamp them in place and drill for the fastening holes. It is best to have them on whatever face of the mould is going directly

The Building Jig

onto the mould position line (Figure 39). Once this is done, clamp the mould to the fillet and use a plumb line or vertical level to make sure that the mould is vertical across the strongback (Figure 40). If it is not, adjust to suit and finally drill holes to take the fastenings. Bolt everything together and check in all three planes. Slack off the bolts and use thin shims to make any adjustments necessary, then go onto the next mould.

Once all the moulds have been erected, check all the moulds against each other. Eye the whole structure up and make sure that nothing looks wrong. If it does, check back to the jig drawing. Any stem/stern formers must be erected with the same care. In canoe construction where there usually is a stem and stern former, it often best to erect these first and then to stretch a string between them which is exactly on the centreline of the hull. This will be directly above the centerline marked on the strong back and can be used as a further reference to make sure that the moulds are not erected leaning over to one side. If the canoe or dinghy has some rocker to the bottom then this line may need to be fastened to two 'posts' screwed to the side of the stem and stern formers so that it clears the bottom line (Figure 41).

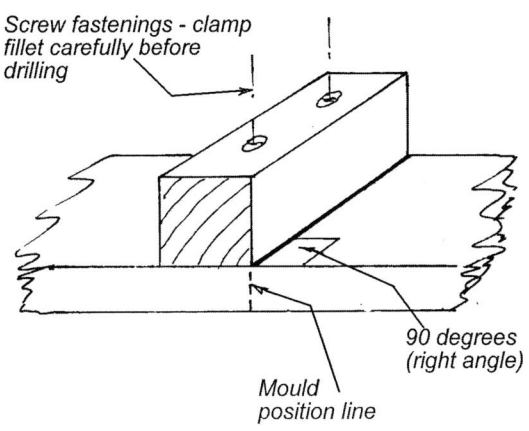

Fig 39. Using simple wood fillets to attach the moulds directly to the strong back.

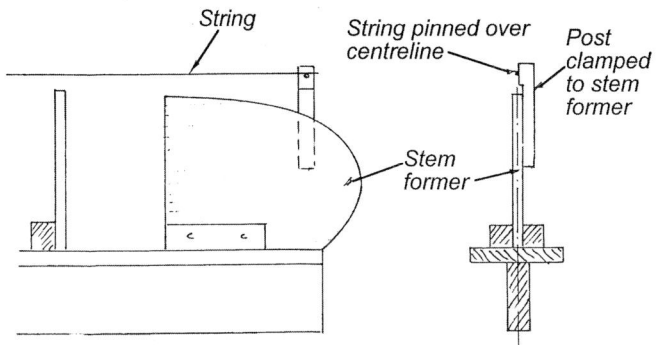

Fig 41. Using a string to help set up the centerline on a canoe or dinghy jig.

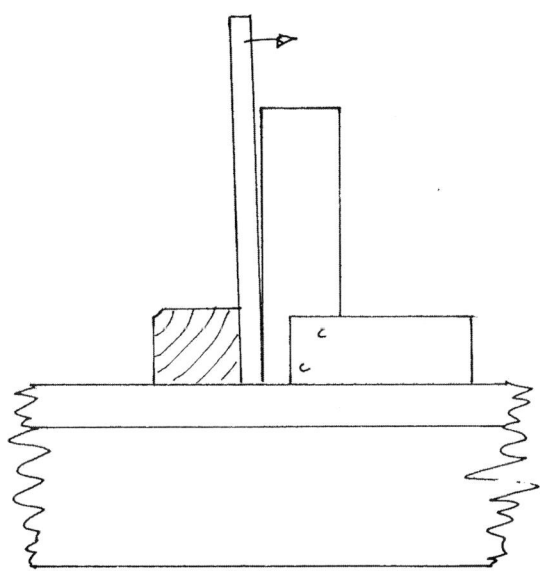

Fig 40. Use a square (or plumb line) to check that the moulds are vertical to the strong back.

Above—substantial supports and strong back being used on this 23'3" Frigate's Boat by the Historical Maritime Society.

The Building Jig

Three pictures of Anders Linderberg's 15' Felix launch. In this case he has set up each mould on a headstock the height for which has been taken from the mould dimensions.

Note on the bottom picture how blocks have been used between the moulds to help brace them—he has started planking from the gunwale and the edges of the moulds have been taped so that the planking does not stick to them.

Chapter 3
INTERNAL HULL STRUCTURE

3.1 General

Some of the internal structure (and in some cases, most of the internal structure), may be fitted before the planking commences. You do need a centreline member of some sort to define the centreline of the boat and this will at least consist of some form of internal stem along with a hog (although in canoes this is often omitted). The hog runs the length of the boat from the stem post to the stern post or transom (Figure 42).

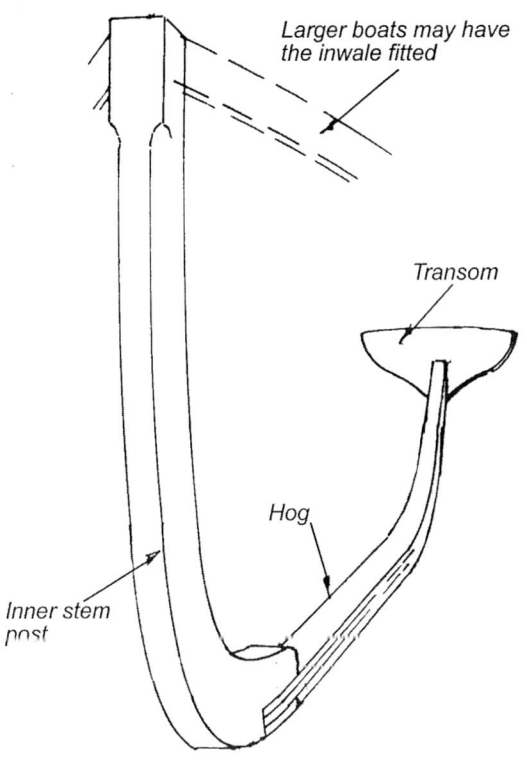

Fig 42. The inner keel (hog), stem and transom assembly.

In boats with a transom you will also need to erect the transom itself of course, or for double ended boats there will be a stern post similar to the stem. Additionally, larger boats may have the inwale fitted. This is temporarily fastened to the moulds so that the fastenings can be removed, but permanently glued and fastened to any other permanent structure ie., stem post and transom. The inwale will define the sheer line of the boat but fitting it before the planking, does mean that it is more difficult to remove the hull from the jig and in order to do this, the moulds have to be split and be removable from the strong back. From this point of view, it is often better to fit the inwale after the hull has been removed from the jig (the exception may be larger boats which will need some form of strength member at the deck edge when the hull is rolled over).

Sometimes, transverse floors and frames are fitted before planking starts. In this case these members are temporarily fastened beside the moulds. The floors can be glued up from 'lifts' of hardwood and screwed beside the mould (Figure 43). The 'faying' surface between the floor and the planking is then bevelled at the same time as the edges of the moulds are bevelled. The planking is glued and fastened directly to the floors.

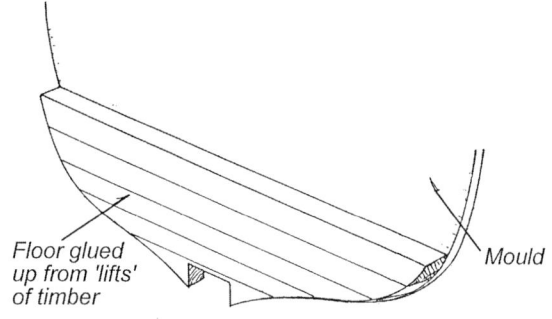

Fig 43. Gluing up the floors beside the moulds.

3.2 Internal Stem/Stern Post

This may be a temporary chipboard former of the stem shape which is part of the building jig or it may be a permanent internal stem. Generally, canoes use a temporary chipboard former and the inside of the stem is strengthened by an epoxy fillet, several layers of glass tape or a laminated wood stem piece. A good way of making up a laminated wood stem, is to make up a chipboard former for the stem and then to remove the depth (moulding) of the laminated stem from it. The internal stem is then laminated directly onto the chipboard stem mould before this is fastened to the strong back (Figure 44).

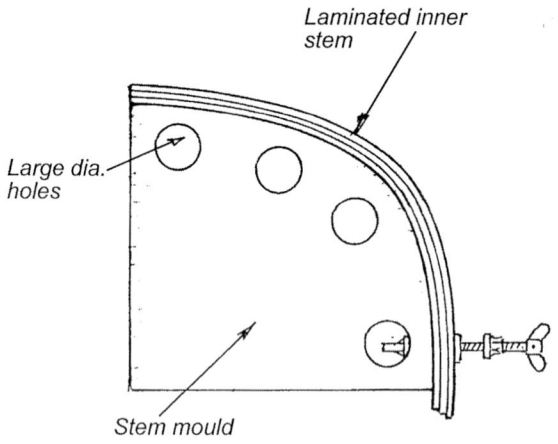

Fig 44. Laminating a canoe inner stem.

A laminated internal stem for a canoe may be 3/4" (18mm) wide (sided) and 3/4" (18mm) deep (moulded) and can be made up from three strips of 6mm x 18mm hardwood. The strips will need to be 'steamed' in order to make them supple enough to bend around the stem mould. If a steam box is not available, simply soak them overnight in hot water. Next day soak them for a further hour or two in hot water and then clamp them over the edge of the mould. The mould can have large holes cut close to it's edge to allow you to use clamps to hold the strips in place. Hold the mould in a vice as you do this and leave clamped for a day.

The strips will need to dry and this may take up to 2 or 3 days. When they are dry, they can be removed and glued together again clamped to the mould. Put masking tape over the edge of the mould so that the strips do not get glued to the mould by any stray glue.

A crude form of steam box can be made by using a piece of drain pipe or even heavy cardboard tube. Seal the top of the tube and put the strips inside. Clamp the tube vertically with it's lower open end over the spout of a boiling kettle. Seal around the opening into the tube with rags to keep the steam in the tube. After 30 minutes or so, the wood should be supple enough to bend and will take less time to dry out before it can be glued.

On larger craft, the internal stem will be a bigger affair and can be laminated separately by making up a chipboard former. This may take the form of a chipboard shape cut to the shape of the 'outside' of the internal stem with another former representing the interior shape of the stem. The outer shape can be fastened to a board and after the strips for the stem have been steamed or soaked they can be forced into place by clamping the interior shape against them trapping them against the outer shape (Figure 45). For larger and heavier stems a similar system is used but may take the form of steel angle brackets bolted to a strong bed.

The stem/stern post may also be made up in conventional fashion from pieces of wood shaped to fit together and glued and bolted. Just as the rest of the moulds are shaped to the 'inside' of the planking, so the stem is

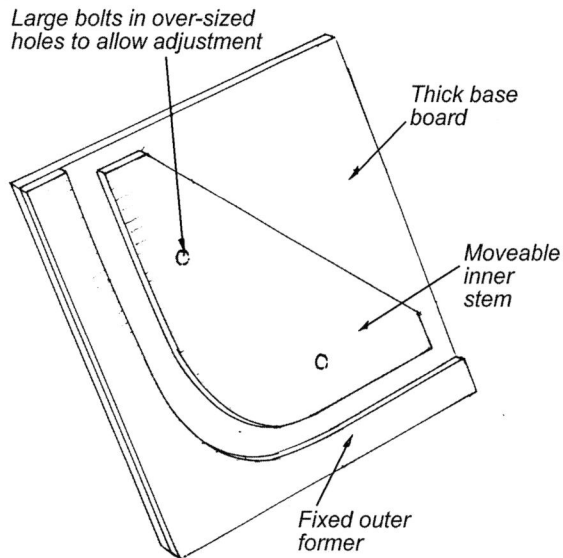

Fig 45. A simple laminating jig for the inner stem on large boats.

also to the 'inside' of the planking. This means that it will need to be bevelled both sides at some stage (Figure 46). This is best done after it has been erected onto the jig when the edges of the moulds are bevelled. If the stem has been made up from pieces of wood bolted together remember to arrange the bolts so that they are clear of the bevelling.

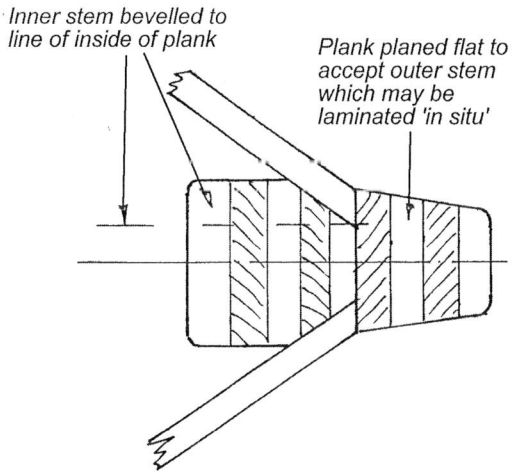

Fig 46. Modern inner and outer stem on a strip planked hull.

3.3 Transom

If the boat has a transom you have to choose between making it up with or without any allowance for bevel along it's edge. There is no reason why the transom cannot be made up out of a simple sheet of plywood cut to the shape of the 'inside' of the plank with the edges of the plywood left square. The planking is then allowed to run out over the edge of the transom and the gap between the planks and the transom edge is then filled with epoxy filleting (Figure 47). Later this filleting is greatly enlarged and perhaps covered with several layers of glass woven roving to make a structural epoxy joint. The disadvantages of this method are the cost of the epoxies and the fact that there is not much to initially attach the planking too (there is only the edge of the ply which is not even bevelled for the planking). The advantage is in speed. If you do use this method, use enough epoxy to hold the planks in place but leave the major part of the fillet and it's glass covering until the hull is turned upright.

The conventional way to construct the transom is to allow for the bevel on it's edge and to fit a wood framework. The framework can be shaped and fastened to the transom so that it overhangs the transom enough to allow for the amount of bevel that will be required. In this case it is a good idea to draw down the angle between the transom and centreline structure full size on a piece of paper and to measure from this the allowance needed for the bevel (Figure 48). The amount of bevel around the transom will change from the bottom to the top. Usually it is most at the bottom of the transom. As with the rest of the structure, great care must be taken when erecting the transom so that it is accurately positioned. The actual bevelling, like that for the stem, may be done on the jig just before planking.

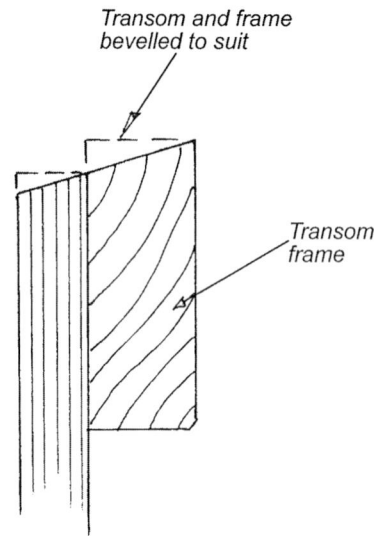

Fig 48. A conventional transom frame.

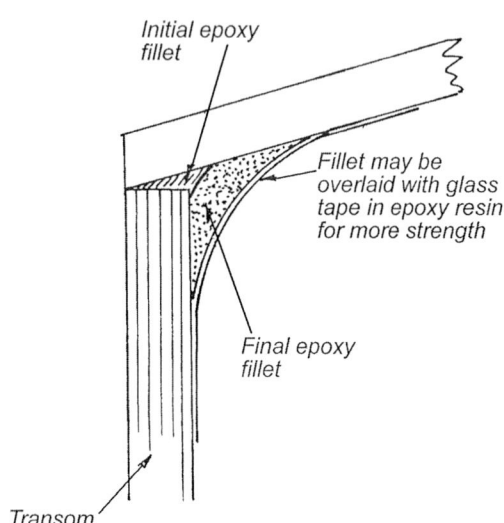

Fig 47. A simple epoxy fillet join between the planking and transom.

3.4 Hog (Internal Keel)

On small boats and canoes, this may not exist although in these cases a central keel plank may be fitted first before the rest of the planking. The disadvantage of a wood hog is that it gets in the way if the inside of the hull is to be sheathed. Internal sheathing is a lot easier if the inside of the boat is completely 'clean'. However, most boats other than canoes and small canoes will have one and it does, of course, define the centreline of the hull. The type of hog fitted will depend upon the size and shape of the boat. Yachts which were originally designed for conventional carvel planked construction will have a complete hog/skeg/deadwood structure and the planking will sit into a rabbet (groove) which has been carefully chiselled into the side of this structure. With strip planking, the keel structure is made up in at least 2 parts. First, the internal keel or hog is fitted and the planking is simply allowed to overlap this (Figure 49). The planking inway of the outside keel/deadwood is then planed flat so that this external structure can be glued and fastened in place. Because the keel is usually always made up from hardwood (for it's weight and strength) and the planking is often made from a softwood (ie. Cedar), the planking which crosses the hog is often 'selected' from the plank stock because it is denser than the rest of the planking. From a batch of Cedar planks you will find some which are 'harder' than the rest and these should be used in way of the centreline structure.

Of course, just how many 'hard' planks will actually cross the hog will depend upon how the planks run over the hull. If the planks 'run' in at an angle over the hog, only their ends will actually go over the hog whilst the remainder of the plank will lay away from the hog itself. But if these planks can be chosen

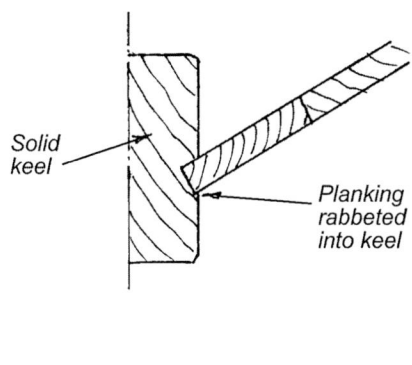

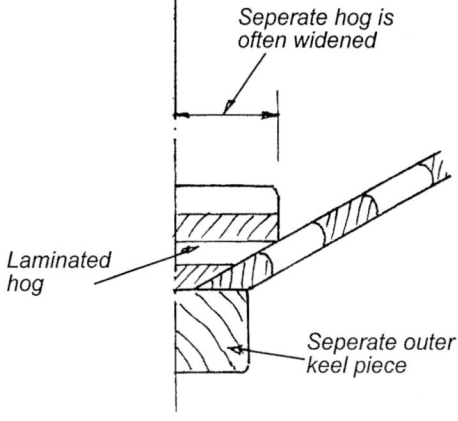

Fig 49. A traditional and modern hog/keel structure.

for their higher density from the rest of the stock, then this will suffice. Those planks which run over the stem and stern can be lower in density. To a certain degree this is all a 'nicety' and you may find that all the planks that have been delivered to you are more or less of equal density.

In converting from conventional carvel planking to strip planking the designer will usually have separated out the keel structure to produce what we call the 'canoe body' form of the hull that is to say, the hull proper will be separate from the external keel rather than being an integral part of it. The internal hog may now follow a different shape from what it used to be in the carvel planked hull. Often, it follows a fairly smooth curve

Internal Hull Structure

between the stem and the stern post or transom. In this case, it can be safely laminated 'in situ' (on the jig) over the moulds. The moulds are modified by having a slot cut out of them to accommodate the hog. The depth of this cut out wants to be carefully marked. It will be the thickness (moulding) of the hog taken from the mould shape as it crosses the centreline. This will leave the upper surface of the hog (actually the lower surface when the boat is upright) to be bevelled either side of the centerline ready for the planking to fit over it (Figure 50).

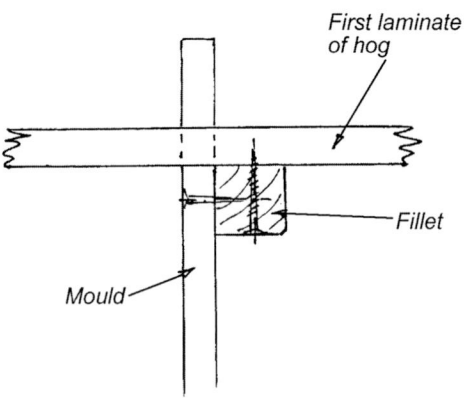

Fig 51. Fixing the first hog laminate to the moulds.

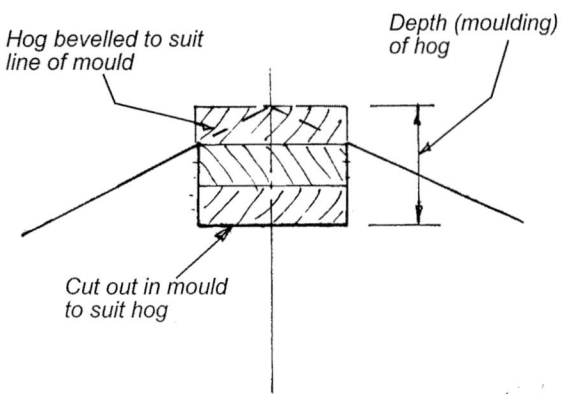

Fig 50. The cut out in the moulds for the hog.

Above—the fantail/counter stern of the Edwardian 26 launch with a combined hog and horn timber being laminated in place. With this type of stern, no matter what size the boat is, the deck line at the stern needs to be defined by an inwale frame. In this case, it has been laminated off the boat.

The hog should be glued together in thin enough laminations so that it bends 'in place' without distorting the moulds. Screw wood blocks to one face of the moulds with their upper surfaces level with the slot cut for the hog. Screw up through these blocks into the first lamination to hold it in place. Subsequent layers are simply glued in place using screws between the layers to hold in place. Use plenty of glue and make sure that the screws used are clear of any area which will be bevelled (Figure 51).

Usually the hog is 'let' into the internal stem/stern and will have a knee to connect it to any transom (Figure 52).

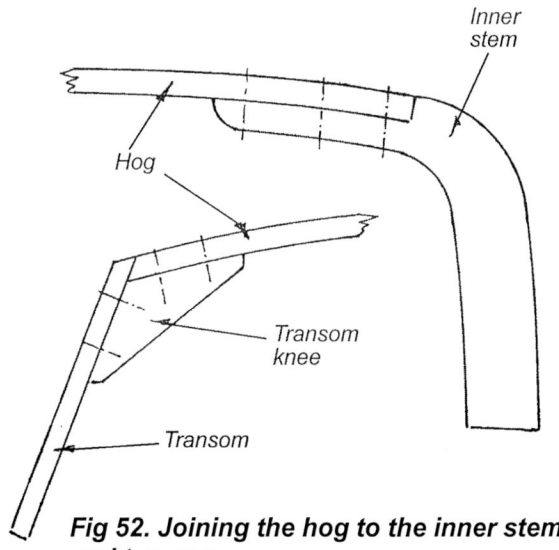

Fig 52. Joining the hog to the inner stem and transom.

3.5 Floors & Frames

A floor is an athwartships (from side to side like a frame) structural item which ties the 2 halves of a frame together across the centerline of the boat (Figure 5). It considerably strengthens the bilge area of the hull and often has the ballast keel bolts passing through it. In many boats they are quite an important part of the internal structure over the middle half of the boat where they are also 'tied' in with the engine bearers. In traditional construction, they were positioned at almost every frame over most of the boat length.

As we have already mentioned, floors may be made up from 'lifts' (square sectioned timber) of hardwood. Having glued up sufficient lifts to give the depth required, the floor can be positioned against it's supporting mould and marked. Remove it, cut to shape and screw to the mould (Figure 53). When the edges of the moulds and the stem, hog etc are bevelled, the floors can be bevelled at the same time. Floors are not particularly easy items to fit accurately into the bottom of a hull shell and therefore, erecting them before planking the hull, will make this process easier and you will get a close fit between the floors and the planking much easier.

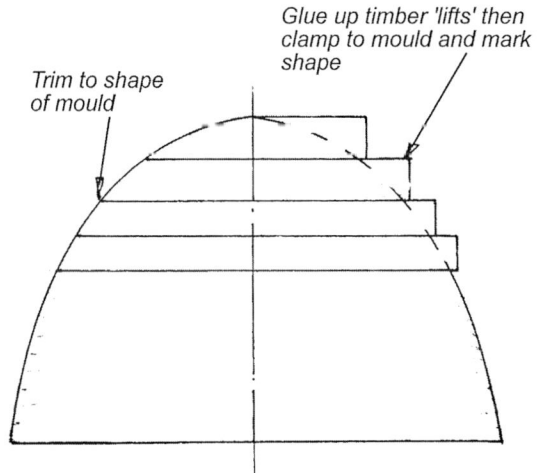

Fig 53. Using a mould to gain the shape of the floor.

The contribution that a floor makes to the strength of the boat depends upon how far it reaches out either side of the centreline and upon it's own stiffness. A wood floor gains much of it's stiffness from it's depth (moulding) but a deep floor can get in the way of the accommodation. A solid wood floor made up from 'lifts' will only 'reach' well out either side of the centreline if it is also deep, especially in a narrow gutted deep 'v' hull shape. Hence, the solid floor type may not be appropriate, in which case the floors may need to be laminated 'to shape' (Figure 54). This type of floor may be easier fitted after the hull has been planked when it can be laminated directly into the hull. Metal strap floors will have to be fitted after the planking.

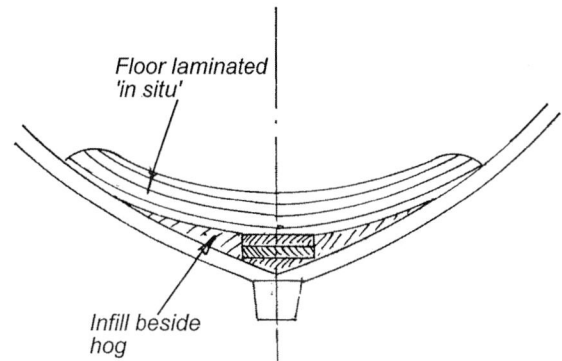

Fig 54. Floors laminated 'in situ'.

Many strip planked hulls do not have any transverse frames. The fact that the hull, especially when it has been sheathed both sides in glass and epoxy or overlaid with diagonal wood veneers, can be considered as a monocoque structure with a single continuous skin, means that much of the job performed by framing is no longer required. However, transverse structure is still required to transfer the keel, rudder, mast and rigging loads. Very often, much of these can be taken by transverse plywood bulkheads which are also positioned to provide partitioning to the accommodation, but, when these bulkheads are too widely spaced or simply do not fall in the correct position to take the loads, intermediate transverse framing may need to be fitted.

In this case, it is often easier to laminate these frames from Oak or Iroko off the boat and to erect these along with the moulds onto the strong back. Obviously, where a frame occurs, there is no need for a mould so that the frames can do two jobs, that of helping to form the hull shape and of being a strength member. If there are any frames in the construction, their shape should be given in the plans, or if you have lofted, they can be taken off the loft floor. Laminating them can be done in much the same way as the stem.

Another way of incorporating the frames is to fit them to the edge of the moulds. This is quite an old way of doing it and is particularly useful in small boats. Although of clinker construction, the Herreshoff dinghy uses this method. The moulds are not shaped to the inside of the planking but to the inside of the frames. The frames are then simply laminated directly onto the edge of the moulds using the moulds to form the frames (Figure 55). The edges of the moulds are covered with tape so that the frames will not stick to them. Herreshoff made up some special clamping irons known as 'framing dogs' to hold the frame laminates in place whilst they are being glued up. You can use the method shown for the inner canoe stem and cut large holes which will allow the use of 'G' cramps to hold the frame laminates in place.

These frames may be in two pieces with each halved either side of the hog. In this case they may be 'checked' into the hog. Alternatively, they may be in one piece and cross the centreline structure. Whichever way they are made, the planking will glued and screwed directly to them. If the frames have floors attached to them then the frame and floor can be fastened together before being erected onto the strongback.

On steam launches I often opt for a hull which is sheathed on the outside but not on the inside. On the interior of the hull I go for a more conventional stiffening system using laminated transverse framing with a conventional substantial bilge stringer and inwale which are fastened over the frames. I use this system, which in many respects is quite old fashioned because of the additional stresses and strains imposed upon the hull by the weight of the steam plant, boiler and bunkers especially if the launch is going to be trailed. On unframed strip hulls, the bilge stringer can be glued directly onto the inside of the hull but it will not give as much stiffness to the hull as a conventional stringer which is separated from the hull by framing. Using a bilge stringer over frames, allows the stringer to act like a continuous 'I' beam with the hull, imparting a lot of stiffness to the hull shell.

The same can be said of the inwale, which is why, very often, an inwale which is attached directly to the hull has to have a larger cross section than one which is separated from the hull by the depth of the frames (Figure 56).

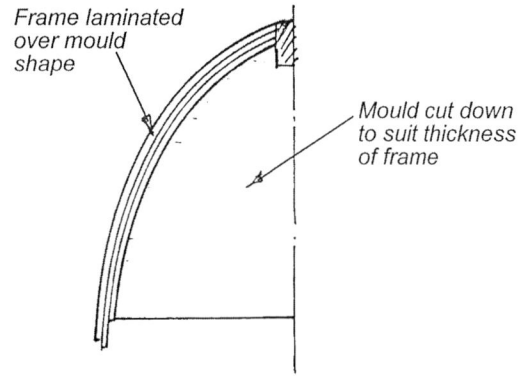

Fig 55. Laminating the frames over the moulds which have been cut down to suit.

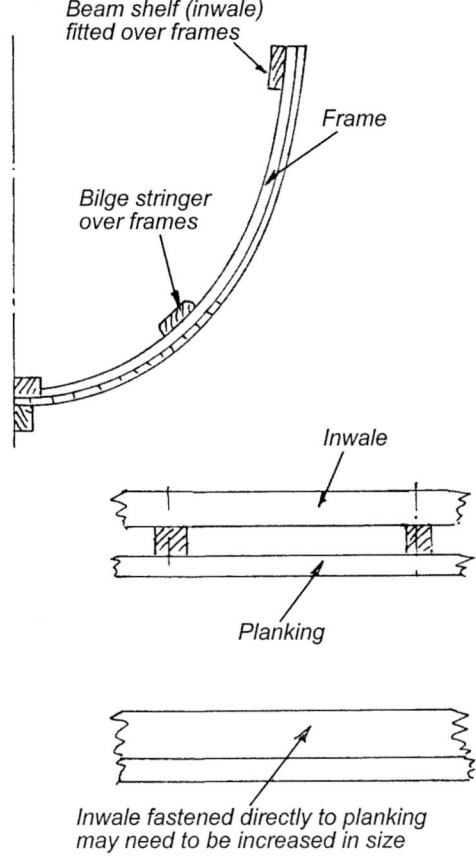

Fig 56. Inwales and bilge stringer fitted over the frames.

accommodated in one of three ways. First, the initial laminate against the hull will simply have to be bevelled and fitted to the hull surface so that the frame is at 90 degrees to the centerline of the boat. This takes time but once the first laminate has been bevelled and fitted, the remaining laminations can be planted straight onto it with no further work. The second method is not to bevel the frame at all but to leave a gap which will then be filled with thickened epoxy. A compromise can be made between the first two methods with some bevelling done and the remainder of the gap filled with epoxy (Figure 57).

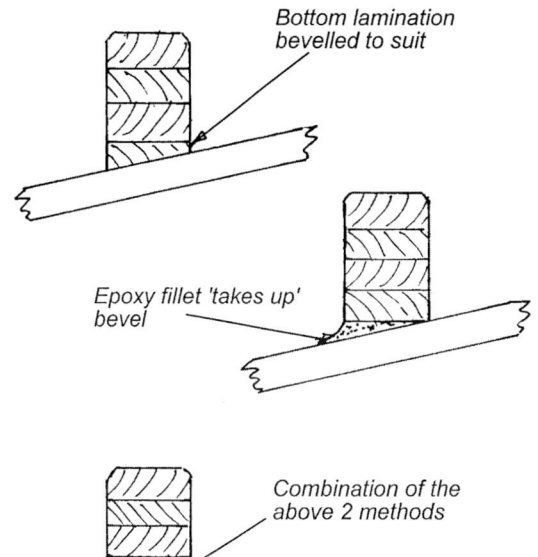

Fig 57. Laminating the frames.

Hence, on strip planked steam launches I often incorporate a system of Oak frames which are laminated 'in situ' after the hull has been removed from the jig. One thing to remember is that any fastening which is to be done through the hull into items such as stringers should be done before any sheathing is applied to the outside. The sheathing should cover all such fastenings which may mean that the hull will need turning over on at least two occasions.

Frames laminated in the middle portion of the boat will fit fairly well, directly onto the hull skin but frames towards the ends of the boat will have to contend with the bevel imposed by the curve of the hull. This can be

The third method is to 'cant' the frames. In other words, they may be fitted flat against the inside of the hulls surface which means that they will not be at 90 degrees to the centreline. There is no real reason why this should not be done and it can be argued that, by fitting the frames to this 'natural' route, they will impart more stiffness and strength to the hull, being at 90 degrees to the hull

Internal Hull Structure

surface and therefore absolutely in the right direction to oppose deflection to the hull. The forces of buoyancy imparted to the hull by the surrounding water do not act at 90 degrees to the centerline but at 90 degrees to the hull surface. The reasons for not using cant frames throughout the boat are partly one of aesthetics and also because frames are often used to tie bulkheads to. However, very often, and especially in hulls with very curvaceous ends, the frames are canted just over the last few metres at the bow and stern anyway where they are clear of bulkheads and out of sight (Figure 58).

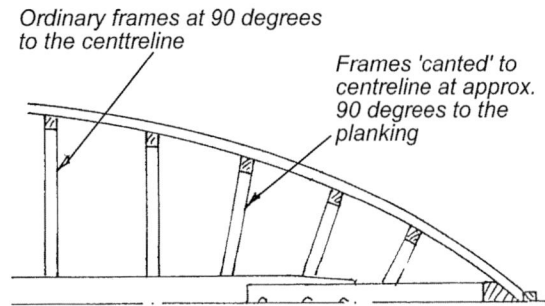

Fig 58. Ordinary and cant frames.

Overall, transverse frames are used less and less now in strip planked construction with the advent of more efficient glues. Before epoxies became available, strip planking was nailed together and was also backed up by a system of small bent or laminated frames. Typically, a 25ft (7.6m) yacht would have 18mm strip planking and 1"x1" (25x25mm) frame at 12" (305mm) centres. The planking may have been nailed at 3" (76mm) centres. These scantlings are more or less to Lloyds for conventional carvel planked hulls and make no allowance for the benefit gained from having a monocoque hull structure where the glue joints between the planking are stronger than the planking itself. But it is a mistake to leave transverse framing out where it may be needed to transmit loads from keels etc.—the pictures on this page show other approaches to fitting them.

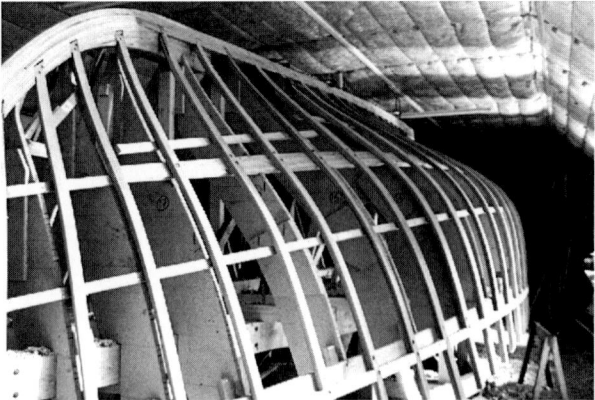

Above and below—Iain Tolhurst's Pinky Ketch—in this case the moulds were reduced in size by the thickness of the bilge stringer and inwale—these were fitted along with several temporary stringers and the frames laminated over the top. Towards the bow and stern you can see how the frames 'cant'.

Below—Peter Brittijn's Ijssel launch is built in much the same way as the Pinky except that the frames have been laminated directly on top of the moulds—the bilge stringer was laminated first and fitted into slots cut into the moulds.

Chapter 4
MATERIALS FOR STRIP PLANKING

4.1 The Planking

There are at least three sections of plank used for strip planking – square edged, cove/convex (bead and cove) or tongue and groove (Fast Strip/Speed Strip etc). There are advantages and disadvantages to using each in terms of cost, ease of use, time saving etc.

4.1.2 Square Edged

Square edged planking is going to be easier to obtain in that it requires no special machining. Because it does not need any special machining (apart from that required to make it smooth) it will be cheaper than the planking which has been specially put through a milling machine to give it the cove/convex edge shape. Also, in shaping the edges, you do loose width and instead of a 25mm plank being just that, with a shaped edge you will loose around 5 or 6mm of width. Losses will depend upon the thickness of the planking (if the same radius of curve is used no matter how thick the plank, the wider plank will have a greater depth of curve taken from it). This means the use of more planks and yet again more expense (Figure 59). The depth of the concave shape on an average piece of 18mm thick plank may be 4mm. Very often, the radius used on the convex edge of the plank is slightly greater than on the concave edge so that a small gap is left for the glue in the centre of the plank join and the edges of the concave piece are pressed tight against the mating piece of plank. This effect is very slight and should not be over done especially since, on a tightly curved bilge area, the planking will not sit well together as the inside edge tries to 'dig' into the adjacent plank.

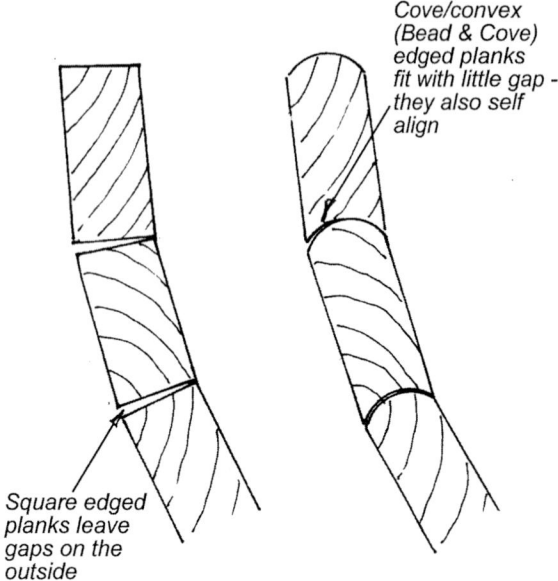

Fig 59. *Square edged and Cove/Convex (Bead & Cove) sectioned planks.*

Furthermore, on 'normal' hull shapes on boats of 24' or more, the actual gap that you get on the outside of the planking where one planks meets another, is not very great and this gap simply becomes filled with the epoxy glue. The depth of this gap will depend upon the thickness of the planking, but especially in the case of a hull which is going to be double diagonal planked with veneers on the outside, the strip planking may be quite thin and therefore square edged timber will have less of a gap to fill. Also, because the strip planking is going to be covered, it may seem senseless to go to the expense of using cove/concave edged planking which is going to be hidden anyway. I have to say that on the steam launches that I have been involved in of 24' or more in length, the hull shape has been such that very little gap on the outside of the planking was left to fill. Hulls with relatively slack bilges will have very little in the way of gaps between the planks. On the other hand, hulls which have tight bilges (a lot of tight curvature in the bilges) will show more gaps between the planks.

To avoid any gap in the outside of the plank seams, the top of each plank can be 'dressed' before the next plank goes on (Figure 60). This simply entails 'fitting the next plank by offering it up on to the hull and measuring the gap at various positions along the length of the plank. This gap is then planed off the 'inside' of either the plank already in place or the one being fitted to give a snug fit between the 2 planks. Rather than have to offer the whole plank up each time that you gauge the amount to be 'dressed off', use a short length of scrap planking at each mould station, gauge the amount to be removed, plane it off and then connect up the planed areas in between.

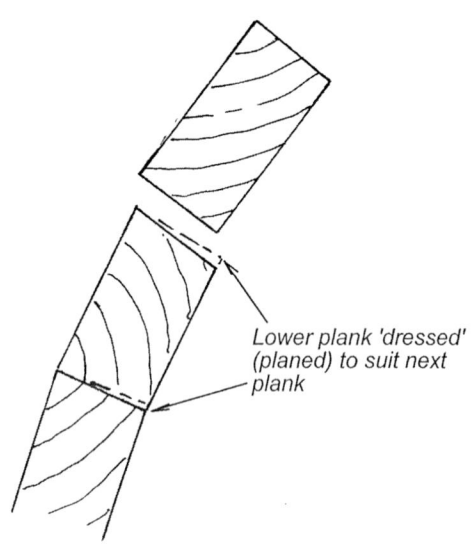

Fig 60. *'Dressing' square edged planks.*

4.1.2 Cove/Convex (Cove and Bead)

Having seemingly argued for using square edged planking, there are big advantages when using planking with cove/convex shaped edges. The first, is that the trough presented by the plank which you are about to glue to, with a new plank, will hold the glue nicely without letting it drip down the hull sides. It is surprising just how much this saves in the amount of glue which is wasted. There is nothing worse, than to apply the glue to the plank edge and to get to the far end only to see it running in great torrents down the hull side, to be wasted on the workshop floor (or to glue your boots down!). Secondly, and this is quite an important point, the cove/convex shaped planks are more or less self aligning. With one plank fitting snugly into the other, there is less chance of misalignment along the plank. A misalignment of only 0.5 of a millimetre may seem insignificant, but when it is over a length of perhaps 25' it creates a lot more work to plane it down or to fill the surface. Care in aligning the planks is essential and cove/convexed edged planks make this easier. In gluing the planks together, you only need to worry about the clamping pressure between each plank and it's vertical alignment and not the sideways alignment between the planks. I have found that prices do vary dramatically around the country so it is worth getting several quotes from timber suppliers for both square edged stock and for the cove/convex stock.

4.1.3 Tongue & Groove (Speed Strip/fast Strip etc)

As the use of Strip Planking for hulls has progressed at least one other machined shape has been introduced - this a "tongue and groove" machined timber. In the UK there are at least two companies, Jos. Thompson & Co. Ltd and Robbins Timber Ltd who have introduced this type of machined Cedar into their supply catalogues.

In Thompson's case it is known as "Speed Strip" and in Robbins case it is known as "Fast Strip". both companies say that these strips are not simply machined with the usual tongue and groove as this would be too tight and not allow for the need of the wood to lie over a curved section but are machined with special cutters to give a section which is very much self aligning but allows use over a compounded surface. I have used both of these products and find them excellent (Figure 61).

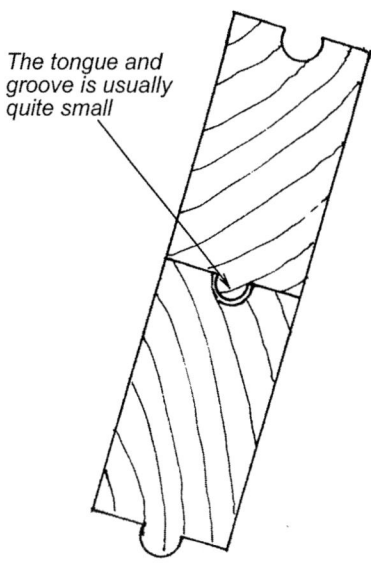

Fig 61. Tongue and groove sectioned planks.

Advantages of this type of strip are :-

Planks are easier to self align requiring much fewer fastenings or clamps to hold the planks in place.

Due to the above, the planking process is much quicker and on bigger boats requires much less labour - a real consideration when labour costs are involved. A better "gutter" for the glue to lie in.

Disadvantages of this type of strip are :-

This type of strip requires much more machining and subsequent waste in wood hence it is often considerably more expensive than square edged and cove/convex strip.

Linked to the above, the sort of thin strip required for canoes which may only be 6mm (1/4") thick is very difficult to machine and often results in a lot of wasteage, hence it's very high cost - the tongue and groove sides tend to break off unless the grain is exceptionally straight.

Changing the direction of planking (Chapter 1 - Figure 11) causes a problem in that you cannot easily have a tapered plank with "tongue and groove" and so for this area the builder needs to revert to planning off the tongue and groove of adjacent planks.

If the section curve is very tight, the planking width needs to be narrower than usual otherwise the tongue and groove will not allow the planking to follow the section curve - this is overcome by using narrower strips in such areas.

Overall, if you can afford it, "Speed" and "Fast" strip are worth using.

4.2 The Species of Wood Used

The wood normally used, no matter whether the planking is going to be covered in veneer of not, is Cedar. This is a stiff straight grained wood which takes glue very well. It is light and therefore ideal as the core material sandwiched between layers of glass/epoxy or hardwood veneers. It is easily dented and therefore it does need to be covered at least on the outside of the hull. It will also splinter quite easily and therefore care needs to be taken when shaping or nailing it. Always drill pilot holes when nailing.

Other woods can be used for the planking. Mahogany, either Brazilian or Honduras is often used for small boats and canoes. I have even seen 2nd grade Deal, used which had plenty of knots, but I would not recommend this. It seems to me, that if you are going to invest quite a lot of time in making up a jig and in the planking of the hull, it is a false economy to use low grade materials for the hull planking. The planking stock should be good straight grained timber and preferably quarter sawn (edge grain) as shown in Figure 62. Moisture content should be down to 8 to 12%. Above this, and if you sheath the planking the moisture could cause problems to the sheathing because it is trapped. I have never, however, come across problems with glass cloth and epoxy resin sheathing, when the moisture content of the wood has been below 10 or 12%.

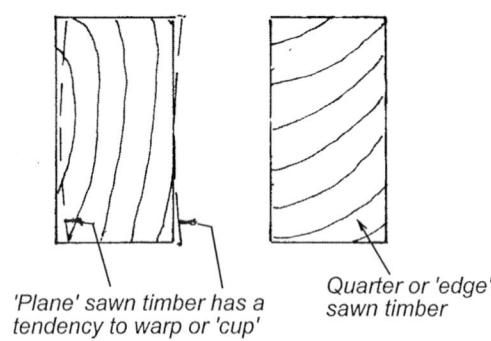

Fig 62. Use quarter (edge) swan timber for the planks.

As I mentioned at the beginning of the manual, because thin strips of wood are used and because each one supports it's neighbour, faults in an individual plank are less critical than in a traditional carvel or clinker constructed hull. This is especially so if the strip planking is going to be sheathed in glass cloth or with hardwood veneers. However, faults should be avoided when selecting the wood as they will inevitably cause more problems when trying to get a good finish on the hull. Knots are of a higher density, than the surrounding wood and therefore when sanding the strip planked hull surface, the sandpaper will cut into the surrounding wood faster than it will into the knotty area. This can lead to quite large 'dips' and hollows which do not become apparent until the hull is being finally coated. Resin pockets in a plank may be filled with epoxy, but again they can adversely effect the finishing of the hull surface.

The wood used for veneering over the strip planking is usually Mahogany in 1.5 to 3mm thicknesses (depending upon the size of the hull). Typically, a 25' hull may be made up from 12mm strip planking with two 2mm veneers on the outside. Do be careful when stripping the hull. It is often thought that the outside veneers will cover up any sins in the strip planking. However, very often, even small bumps and hollows are duplicated through the veneers and appear on the outside.

When you take delivery of the planking stock, do store it carefully, preferably in some sort of horizontal racking system clear of the floor, so that it does not warp or twist. Planking which warps becomes impossible to use.

4.3 Glues

For a while, most modern strip planked hulls were glued together with epoxy glues which were based on thickened epoxy resins (WEST, Structural polymers etc) - epoxy is stronger than the surrounding wood and bonds well to most timbers. However, partly due to it's expense, the fact that it has to be mixed and the difficulty of cleaning epoxy off areas you do not want it to be, many boat builders turned to one of the modern Polyurethane glues, such as Balcotan, for gluing the wood strips together,

Epoxy still needs to be used for the glass sheathing and I would still prefer to use it if I am gluing wood veneers to the outside of the hull.

If you are going to use epoxy to glue the planks together, mixing it in controlled amounts is relatively easy using 'Mini pumps' so that having found out how much will be used per plank, there will be little wastage. Epoxy is expensive when compared with other glues and you want to get well set up for it's use with the correct size mixing containers and spreading devices so as little of it as possible, ends up on the building floor, on you, or in the bin! I have used most of the commonly available brands of epoxy on the market and find little difference between them. My own preference is to use the standard epoxy mixed with a little microfibres to thicken it. The same epoxy or a similar derivative is used for coating the hull surface and also for any glass sheathing so that all the materials are compatible.

Apart from epoxy, other more conventional glues can certainly be used. Before epoxy came on to the boatbuilding scene several different glues were used including Aerolite 306. This is a 2 part glue with the powder part mixed into a paste with water. This is applied to one plank surface (the plank already fastened to the hull) and a hardener is applied to the surface of the plank which is being fitted. The advantage of this type of glue is that it is often cheaper than epoxy and it finishes clear. However, after the 2 planks have met, the working time of the glue is quite short even in comparison to epoxies. So you have to get the new plank lined up and clamped into place quite quickly. I would use fastenings with this type of glue and also with

Aerodux, which is another 2 part resorcinol glue. Aerodux however, dries to a dark brown colour which may not look good with clear finished Cedar planking.

I have seen some strip planked hulls glued together with Cascamite. When brought in quantity, this glue is cheaper still than Aerolite 306 or Aerodux and is simply mixed with water into a creamy paste. After mixing with water it is basically a one part glue. However, it is very brittle after it has cured and does not have the shear strength of either epoxy or Aerolite. It is also not a gap filling glue like epoxy and therefore if it is to be used the planks must be nailed together. One 24' yacht which I saw under construction used low grade Deal planking and Cascamite glue along with galvanized nails. It was obviously a lot cheaper to build than a boat using Cedar planking with epoxy glue and sheathed in glass cloth and epoxy resin. I have to say that I saw this boat out racing during several seasons and although she did not win any races (nothing to do with the materials in her construction), she certainly survived well although her hull surface left a lot to be desired. I simply feel, that if you can afford the difference, then after all the labour that you will put into making an accurate jig and in planking, it will compliment your effort if you use good quality materials. You must also remember the resale value of the boat.

Balcotan 100 has the advantage of being a one component glue. It is a polyurethane glue which cures on contact with moisture. It is used straight out of the container with no preparation or modification and comes in two types, regular and rapid. Regular cures in 4 to 8 hours and rapid cures in 15 to 60 minutes depending upon the temperature. It seems to have fewer possible allergy problems than the epoxies because, unlike the epoxies, it does not contain solvents and gives off little in the way of vapours.

On curing, it expands slightly and will readily fill gaps. This has both an advantage and a disadvantage. It will fill the gaps in square edged planking between the planks which is obviously an advantage. However, it will move or displace a plank if it is not well secured or clamped in place. It is therefore essential to make sure that the planks are not just held in their correct alignment but also, that they will resist the expansion of the glue. This may mean using fastenings, where you would not normally use them, when using epoxy glues. Instead of using edge nailing between the planking, thin strips of plywood can be used up the hull sides which are nailed to each successive plank in order to hold it down whilst the glue sets (see later).

I have seen no real technical literature on it's strength in comparison to epoxies but because of it's foaming/expanding properties I can only assume that it will not have the same shear strength as epoxy and therefore from the cross plank strength point of view, the planking should perhaps be edge fastened on craft over 20' unless the planking is going to be sheathed. Typically, I have seen 22' catamaran hulls built using 8mm Cedar strip and glued with Balcotan 100 sheathed both sides with 400 gm glass cloth in epoxy resin. This will produce a very lightweight but strong skin.

Balcotan 100 has other advantages, not least being the fact that it does not need 'filling' with microfibres etc. It is already a glue, unlike the epoxies which are resins and which therefore need 'filling' before they can be used as glues. 'Filling' an epoxy resin means that it will go less far and partly because of this, you end up using less Balcotan 100 that you would epoxy. Indeed, although not confirmed, you may only use a third of the amount of epoxy, that you would need to use, when using Balcotan. Typically, a 16' Canadian canoe may use 3kg of epoxy resin to glue the planks together, but only 1kg of Balcotan 100.

Cleaning the hull up after planking is also easier. With the epoxies you must clean excess glue off as you go. Any epoxy which cures will cause a headache to remove it. Balcotan 100 on the other hand is much easier. In fact, you do leave any excess to cure and then it is easy enough to remove with a cabinet scraper. It is applied to one surface only and can be easily spread with a serrated spreader. Using Resorcinal glues for strip planking requires good clamping pressure because they shrink as they cure and voids can be left. Balcotan 100 requires good clamping pressure too, but for the opposite reason. It expands and can move a joint out of alignment if sufficient clamping pressure is not applied. Unlike epoxy, Balcotan 100 cannot be used for sheathing the hull with glass fabric. It is purely an adhesive.

4.4 Fastenings

As we have already mentioned, with epoxy glues there really is no need to edge fasten between the planks and even when using non epoxy glues, there is often no real need to fasten at all. Nailing from one thin plank to the other without the nail reappearing embarrassingly through the plank at some point, is not easy. So, getting rid of as many nails as possible from the planking process is an advantage. However, even when using epoxy glues, the occasional nail will help line up the plank properly even when using cove/convex planking and is often the best way of making sure that each plank is sitting tightly against it's adjacent plank.

In an older strip planked hull where the nails formed an important back up to the glue, the nails were often used at 3'' (76mm) centres and they had to be staggered between planks. The width of the planks was often dictated by the length of the nails that were going to be used, as each nail had to go right through one plank and at least three quarters into the adjacent plank to be effective. This meant that for planks 1 1/2'' (38mm) wide the nails had to be at least 2 1/2'' (64mm) long. In my experience, long nails mean bent nails, even with a pilot hole, leaving the pointed tips of the nails squinting at you as they poked just through the planking as they took their own cork screw course! Hence, very often, even on large boats, the planking was just 1'' (25mm) wide which meant more planks, more glue and more labour spent in planking the hull.

If nails are used, then they should if possible be of the bronze barbed ring type (ie. Gripfast) but they are expensive and not always easy to get hold of. Alternatives are galvanized steel nails either of the square sectioned boat type or the weaker wire nail type. Many people use galvanized nails on the basis that they are totally embedded in wood and will therefore not rust. It has to be said, however, that the very act of hammering the nails into the wood will damage the galvanizing and the natural moisture in the wood may then cause rusting. This rust may work it's way to the wood surface and cause unsightly marking or may even effect any sheathing. Nails should have a pilot hole which is equal to half the diameter of the nail when nailing into soft wood and three quarters of the diameter when nailing into hardwood. Nails used for strip construction where epoxy glue has not been used are normally spaced at around four times the thickness of the planking and their length should be at least 1 3/4 times the width of the planking if not more (Figure 63).

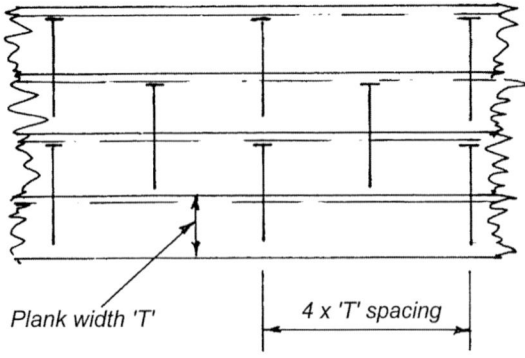

Fig 63. Nail spacing

Where epoxy glues have been used, nails are often omitted altogether or fairly widely spaced at perhaps 1 to 2' (305 - 610mm) centres and these nails are used purely to pull the planking into place and to line it up properly with the adjacent plank. In this case, metal nails are not absolutely essential and some use Nylon nails or wood pegs.

4.5 Sheathing

As we have already mentioned, Cedar especially, is never used without some form of sheathing. The sheathing may of course be a couple of layers of Mahogany veneer which will produce a very strong and impact resistant hull. In some cases the hull may also be veneered inside the hull which will give a true sandwich structure of immense strength. However, veneering on the inside is very difficult and I wonder whether the effort involved is worth it. It would probably be more cost effective to increase the thickness of the Cedar strip slightly or to sheath the inside with glass cloth.

The glass cloth can come in several different types and weights. For canoes and dinghies/dayboats the norm is a simple 6oz (200 gm) woven fabric. For small yachts and launches of around 20' an 8 oz (280 gm) woven fabric can be used and for boats of around 25' in length 10 oz (350 gm) would be used. This is only a very rough guide as the weight of cloth depends upon how much impact strength needs to be incorporated and how much strength and stiffness needs to be added to the strip planking. Obviously, a lightweight strip planking will require more in the way of glass and epoxy to back it up. For instance a 20' or 24' hull made up from 8mm Cedar strip rather than the more usual 18mm would have a layer of 14 oz (450 gm) bi-axial sewn glass fabric both sides of the Cedar. The bi-axial cloth has the bundles of glass filaments laid over each other rather than woven. The bundles are then kept in place by sewing them together. The glass filaments lay flat and because they are not woven (and are therefore not bent) bi-axial cloth is stronger than the ordinary woven fabric. Obviously, the bi-axial cloth is more expensive than the woven fabric and this needs to be taken into account. In the heavier sewn grades quad-axial is also available with filaments laid at 90 degrees and at 45 degrees.

Epoxies are really the only resins which can be used to bond the fabrics to the hull and in this case, the lower viscosity resins should be used so that the fabric is completely 'wetted out'. Structural Polymers have their SP320 Spacote which is a multi purpose resin but which is less viscous than the normal bonding/filleting grade of resin (SP106). WEST use the same resin but have a thinner hardener for use when sheathing. I would not recommend the use of polyester resins (normal fibreglass resins) for sheathing strip planked hulls. These resins simply do not have the strength or the bonding power of the epoxy resins.

4.6 Material Quantities

Now here is a problem! Estimating the amount of wood, resins and adhesives that you will use is rather like asking how long is a piece of string. Not that the quantities are endless, but simply that they are difficult to tie down! The amount of resin that is required for glueing or sheathing will depend upon the porosity of the wood surface, the width of planking, the size of gaps to be filled, whether you are using square edges timber or cove/convex shaped, the temperature and the amount of wastage. I have seen two different people build the same boat using the same method and scantlings and for one to use almost twice the amount of resin as the other. So do be warned, the following figures and methods of calculation are very much 'ball park' figures and methods. Take them as a guide only.

However, there is very little in the way of published literature on material estimates for strip planking and you do need to have some sort of guide for costing and ordering purposes so we will look at several examples. I have partly used the resin manufacturer's own coverage guides and my own experience for these figures.

4.6.1 Planking (incl. glue)

The calculation for the amount of planking is the most simple and usually works out fairly reliable. Unlike liquid resin it is pretty much fixed, the main variable coming in the amount that you allow for wastage. You obviously need to know the surface area of the hull, or at least the bit of it (excluding the transom and deadwood/keel) which is going to be strip planked. The simplest and roughest way to do this is to measure the girth of the boat at the widest and biggest section and multiply this by the length of the boat. This can be measured from the drawings. You will realise that this is only a rough estimate, simply because it assumes that the girth of the hull does not change from the middle of the boat to the ends. Obviously, the girth at the ends of a boat is less, usually, than at the middle and therefore this calculation would be an over estimate. However, I have found in practice that it is not too far out because the difference in girth between the ends and the middle of the canoe body of the hull (the hull without the keel and deadwood etc) is not always that great, especially as the sheer tends to rise towards the ends of the boat and this nullifies some of the decrease in hull width here. Also, the plank length around the greater part of the body of the hull is more than the overall length of the boat, so that the plank length might actually be 31 1/2' (9.75m) for a 30' (9.14m) boat.

A more accurate method is to cut the hull up into a number of sections which are equally spaced. Each section needs to be drawn out and then the girth at each station measured (using a piece of string laid around the shape). These girth lengths are then added together and the total multiplied by the distance between two sections (the section spacing). Because of the way that the bilge area bulges out, multiply this figure by 1.25 (the bilge factor).

So we have :- (Total of all the girths) x (section spacing) x 1.25 = area of hull.

Having gained the total area of the hull surface which is to be strip planked we can, knowing the width of the strip planking to be used, calculate the total length of planking required. As an example, if the total surface area of the hull to be strip planked is 150 sq.ft. and the width of the planking which is going to be used is 1'' then all we have to do to get the total length of plank required, is to divide the hull surface area by the plank width. Do be careful when you divide, that all figures are in the same units, ie. if the area is in square feet, then the figure for the plank width should be in feet (and not inches).

So, our plank length would be 150 sq.ft divided by 1/12 ft. = 150/.0833 = 1800 ft. In metric terms, this would be 13.95 sq.m divided by 25/1000m = 558m.

This quantity of planking is not going to be enough. No allowance has been made for scarfing plank lengths together and for wastage. Also, as previously mentioned, a 50mm wide plank which has cove/convex edging will not give you an effective 50mm wide plank, but something less than that. It may seem excessive, but the wastage factor used is often 25% of the total plank length previously calculated. Hence, for our hull with a surface area of 150 sq.ft, the total length of planking that we should order is 1800 x 1.25 = 2250 ft. This wastage factor is often reduced by professional yards, down to 8 or even 5% in some cases, but this does not take account, in our calculation, for the losses due to concave/convex planks. If you work hard to save material and use some butt joins in the plank lengths, you may be able to get the wastage factor down to say 10-15% (we shall use a wastage factor for the planking of 25% and you can adjust it accordingly).

Having calculated the total length of plank required, we now need to make an estimate of the amount of glue required to glue the planks together. This is the first area where the quantity of material calculated is purely a guide and may vary considerably. Assuming that you do not skimp on the amount of glue that you use and do not end up with voids in the glue line, the amount of glue used will depend upon the plank thickness, the plank width (which dictates the number of glue lines required), the length of the planking used, how big any gaps are in the planking, the working temperature, the density of the wood used and it's porosity and the amount of glue which is allowed to go to waste. With this number of components, some of which can be calculated and some of which are totally variable, it is difficult to gain a definitive figure for the amount of glue required, but we will try!

The figures that follow are based upon the use of standard epoxy resin filled out with microfibres into a 'ketchup' consistency. If you use Balcotan 100 glue, the quantity may be between 33 and 50% of the amount calculated.

Based upon my own experience with strip planking and confirmed from various figures gained from overseas sources, I have come up with a glue requirement factor based upon 1/2" (6mm) thick planking. This is that 1kg of epoxy resin will glue together a 340' length of 6mm thick planking. It may seem that basing all our calculations on the requirements of what must be a small boat, is going to be inaccurate for much larger boats using wider planking. In fact, I have found that the quantities calculated by using this factor on boats up to 30' is fairly accurate. Above that length, it is difficult to be sure, but it will still give a guide.

You can immediately see that if the plank width is 1/2" (12mm), the length of plank that can be glued with 1kg of resin is 340' divided by 12/6 or 340/2 = 170'.

So let us look at some typical examples, calculating both the amount of plank required and the quantity of epoxy glue.

A/. 16' Canadian canoe using 3/4'' x 1/4'' (18x6mm) plank.
Hull surface area = 16' x 4'6'' = 72 sq.ft.
Plank length required = (72 divided by 3/4'' /12) x 1.25 = 1440' (439m).
Glue required = 1440 divided by 340 = 4kg. (In many cases, this may be too much and some canoe builders have used only 3kg).

B/. 16' Open Dayboat/Dinghy using 3/4'' x 1/4'' (18x6mm) plank.
Hull surface area = 16' x 6' = 96 sq.ft.
Plank length required = (96 divided by 3/4'' /12) x 1.25 = 1920' (586m).
Glue required = 1920 divided by 340 = 6kg.

C/. 18' Open Dayboat(heavy) using 3/4'' x 3/8'' (18x9mm) plank.
Hull surface area = 18' x 9' = 162 sq.ft.
Plank length required = (162 divided by 3/4'' /12) x 1.25 = 3240' 988m).
Glue required = (3240 divided by 340) x 9/6 = 14kg.

D/. 21' Trailer Sailer using 1''x3/4'' (25x18mm) plank.
Hull surface area = 20' x 10'6'' = 210 sq.ft.
Plank length required = (210 divided by 1'' /12) x 1.25 = 3163' (965m).
Glue required = (3163 divided by 340) x 18/6 = 28kg.

E/. 26' Steam Launch using 1 1/4''x3/4'' (30x18mm) plank.
Hull surface area = 26' x 10'6'' = 273 sq.ft.
Plank length required = (273 divided by 1 1/4'' / 12) x 1.25 = 3281' (1000m)
Glue required = (3281 divided by 340) 18/6 = 29kg.

These figures compare quite well with actual amounts used but what do we do if the hull has Cedar strip plank covered by a couple of layers of Mahogany veneer. This is simply a matter of calculating the glue requirements for the actual thickness of strip planking used and then adding to this an amount for the veneers. First of all, having cleaned the outside of the Cedar planking up, the surface of the hull will be coated with an initial impregnation coat of epoxy. Again, depending upon the porosity of the wood surface you will need 1.3kg (2.9 lb) of epoxy to coat 100 sq.ft (9.3 sq.m.). The actual gluing of the veneers to the hull will take around 3kg (6.6 lb) of epoxy per 100 sq.ft.

Using these figures for how ever many layers of veneer you are to use, will give the total additional epoxy glue requirement. Whilst it is usual to initially impregnate the Cedar planking, it is not usually necessary to do this with the hardwood veneers so you do not have to allow for the initial impregnation on the underside of the veneers.

4.6.2 Glass Sheathing

Whether or not the hull surface of the Cedar strip hull is veneered, it will almost certainly be sheathed in glass cloth and epoxy so we need to calculate the materials for this process. The amount of glass cloth to be used is a fairly easy calculation knowing the hull surface area. You need to remember if the hull is to be sheathed just on the outside or on both sides.

Woven cloth often comes in 60" wide (1.52m) wide rolls and as an example, if the hull surface area is 200 sq.ft you would divide this figure by 60/12 to gain the length of cloth required. In this case, this would be 40'. The cloth is normally laid on in strips from the gunwale down to the keel unless the hull is quite small (for instance a canoe or small dinghy) when it would be advantageous to lay it on fore and aft to cover the area with the fewest seams. Often specialist fabrics like the quad-axial are specified to be put on over the hull in a specific direction and when calculating the length required you should take this into account. You must also make allowances for overlap and the inevitable wastage. The allowance may be around 20%, so this will need to be added to the figure and our length requirement would go from 40' to 48'. On some boats the waste factor may be much higher. For instance, on a small boat with a half girth from the gunwale to the centreline of the hull bottom of just 3' you will either loose a roughly 18" wide strip if you wanted the cloth to overlap on the centreline or you would have the overlap half way up the other side of the hull. So do not simply use the hull surface area (which may have to be increased if you are to sheath the transom) and allow for some wastage, but think carefully how the fabric is going to be draped over the hull and where the overlaps are going to occur.

Again, we can try and apply a factor for the amount of resin which may be required in the glass sheathing process. First of all, the Cedar needs an initial impregnation coat which we have already calculated as requiring 1.3kg (2.9 lb) of resin (which is unfilled) per 100 sq.ft of hull surface area. This figure is for resin applied with a sponge roller. Second, the factor which I often use for the actual sheathing is (and this takes a bit of mind bending!) 300 sq.ft of 1oz cloth will use 1kg of resin. This is stupid in that nobody uses 1oz cloth. Glass fabric cloth comes in standard weights of 6oz (210gm), 8oz (280gm), 10oz (350gm), 14oz (490gm), 18oz (600gm) and 24oz (800gm). All these weights are per square yard / metre. But using this factor for 1oz cloth over a 300 sq.ft coverage, then we can see that by using 8oz cloth we will be able to cover 300 divided by 8 = 37.5 sq.ft. This assumes that glass fabric uses resin in a linear fashion as it's weight increases, which is probably not correct but I have found that this factor usually works out quite well. A wastage factor of 25% is still applied to the impregnation and sheathing resin.

Apart from the porosity of the wood surface, the amount of resin used for sheathing, will very much depend upon the working temperature of the resin and it's viscosity (thickness). I have found that the normal general purpose epoxy resin is too thick for sheathing purposes and SP Spacote is better. Other manufacturers use different hardeners to alter the viscosity of the working resin.

Materials

Again, let us use the same examples:-

A/. 16' Canadian canoe to be sheathed inside and out.
Surface area = 72 sq.ft x 2 = 144 sq.ft.
For initial impregnation coat - (144 divided by 100) x 1.3 = 1.9kg.
For 6 oz glass sheathing - (144 divided by 300/6) = 2.9kg.
Total is 4.8kg x 1.25 (for wastage) = 6kg.

B/. 16' Open dinghy/dayboat to be sheathed inside and out.
Surface area = 96 sq.ft x 2 x 1.5 (for several large overlaps – large portions of the hull have 3 layers in this particular boat) = 288 sq.ft.
For initial impregnation coat - (288 divided by 100) x 1.3 = 3.7kg.
For 6 oz glass sheathing - (288 divided by 300/6) = 5.8kg.
Total is 9.5kg x 1.25 = 12kg.

C/. 18' Open Dayboat sheathed inside and out.
Surface area = 162 sq.ft. x 2 = 324 sq.ft.
For initial impregnation coat - (324 divided by 100) x 1.3 = 4.2kg.
For 8 oz glass sheathing - (324 divided by 300/8) = 8.6kg
Total is 12.8kg x 1.25 = 16kg.

D/. 21' Trailer Sailer sheathed inside and out.
Surface area = 210 sq.ft. x 2 = 420 sq.ft.
For initial impregnation coat - (420 divided by 100) x 1.3 = 5.6kg.
For 10 oz glass sheathing - (420 divided by 300/10) = 14kg
Total is 19.6kg x 1.25 = 25kg.

E/. 26' Steam Launch sheathed outside and only the bilge area inside.
Surface area = 273 sq.ft. x 1.5 = 410 sq.ft. for sheathing but 273 x 2 = 546 sq.ft. for overall surface impregnation.
For initial impregnation coat - (546 divided by 100) x 1.3 = 7kg.
For 10 oz glass sheathing - (410 divided by 300/10) = 13.7kg.
Total is 20.7 x 1.25 = 26kg.

Remember that these are only ball park figures and of course, the actual amount of resin that you initially order will depend upon the standard sizes of container that the epoxy comes in, these being 1.2kg, 6kg and 30kg. Buying epoxy in small amounts is very expensive. Per kilogram (kg) of epoxy bought in, the largest quantity is around half the cost of the epoxy bought, in the smallest packs. On the other hand you do not want to be left with a large quantity of resin over at the end of the job. However, do remember that you will need further epoxy for the construction and fit out of the remainder of the boat.

I apologize for the rather odd mix of Metric and Imperial measures in the above calculations.

Right—Bob Grutzmacher's 20' Rathlin motor launch planked and being sanded and filled ready to have a layer of diagonal veneer fitted.

Left Wash Kohnke's 28' 6" Corn Bunting turned over and showing the engine beds, bilge stringers and plywood floors fitted—page 4 has a picture of this boat showing the engine beds and bilge stringers fitted before planking commences.

Below is a picture towards the underwater part of the stern for the same hull, beautifully finished and almost ready for the water.

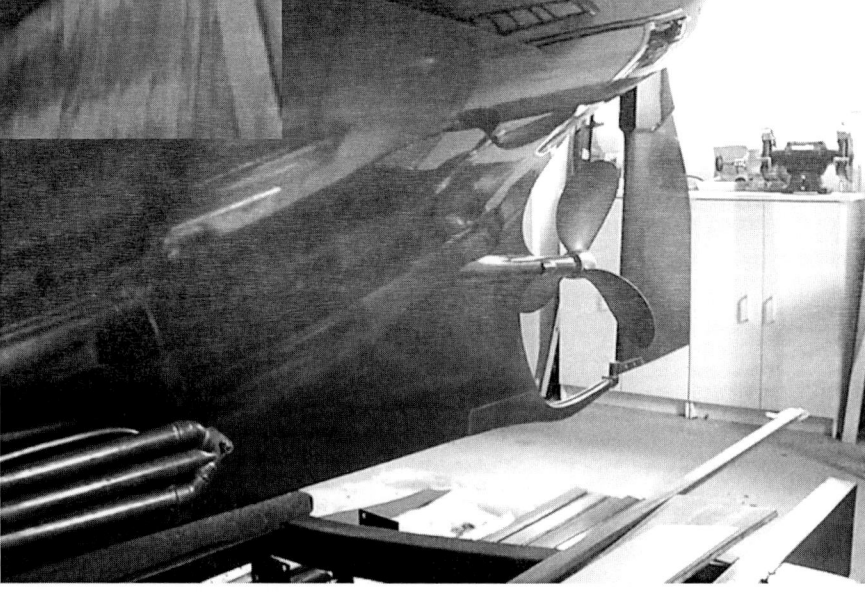

Chapter 5
THE PLANKING PROCESS

5.1 Preparing the Jig

Having erected the moulds onto the strong back and fitted the hog, stem and transom structure into place, the next step is to prepare the jig ready for planking. The main job here is to bevel the edges of the moulds and the backbone structure ready to accept the lay of the planking over it. You will see that the moulds have been positioned on the strong back so that forward of the midship section, the moulds have their aft face on the station position line. The reverse is true of the aft moulds so that the edges of the moulds need to be shaped in order to allow the planking to lie correctly as it goes fore and aft (Figure 36).

First, scarf up one of the plank lengths so that you have a plank batten which is slightly longer than the length of the hull. This plank/batten is then used to gauge the amount of bevel to be planed off the moulds and hog etc. Start by temporarily nailing the plank to the midship mould half way along the girth of the mould, so that it is in the bilge area of the hull. Let the batten lie over the planks in a relaxed manner allowing it to take it's own route fore and aft roughly half way up each mould. By doing this you will see how much bevel is required in the area of the batten at each mould. The midship mould will probably require no bevelling at all. Start at the moulds just fore and aft of the midship mould and plane the bevel to suit over a 3"-6" (75-150mm) portion of the mould edge (Figure 64).

Work your way fore and aft to the next moulds doing the same eventually getting to the stem and transom. Do the same here and then work back making sure that you have

The Planking Process

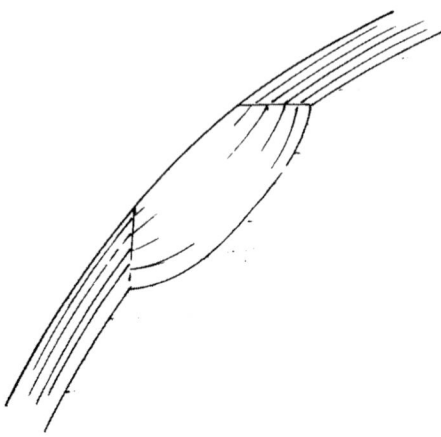

Fig 64. Plane a bevel 'hollow' over a length of 3-6" (75-150mm) to suit the lay of the batten.

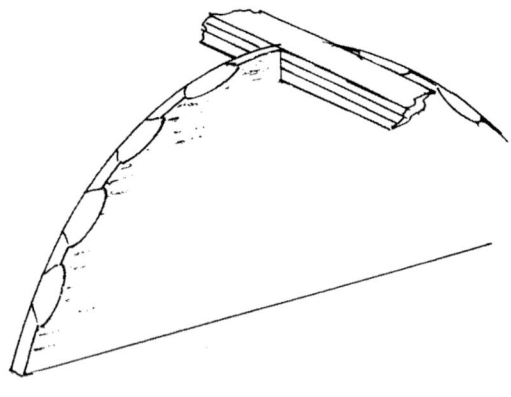

Fig 65. Several 'hollows' planed along the edge of the mould.

removed enough bevel at each mould and that the plank/batten is lying flat on the edge of each mould and is following a fair curve with no lumps or bumps in it.

If there is any unfairness in the curve of the batten, leave it for now until you have done all the bevelling. Remove the nail and re-position the plank/batten 6''-9'' (150-225mm) further up or down from the first batten position and repeat the process. Do this on both sides of the hull and all along the edge of each mould from hog to gunwale. You will end up with a series of hollows on the edge of each mould to one side, and on the backbone structure (Figure 65). For the hog and to a certain extent, the stem, continue the line of the mould up, bevelling the backbone as you go (Figure 50). You can now plane the remaining material off between the hollows and then use the batten again to check that all the components are correctly bevelled.

If any unfairness in the lie of the plank/batten at any mould does occur, then before you do anything active about it, check back with the drawings or lofting to make sure that a mistake has not been made in marking out the mould. Unfairness will show if the plank lies clear of a mould or is obviously pushed out by the mould into an unfair curve. If the unfairness occurs on one side only then there will probably be an obvious problem in the marking out of the mould. If there is a hollow in the lie of the plank/batten then the moulds either side of the offending mould will have to be carefully planed down or additional material applied to the edge of the undersized mould.

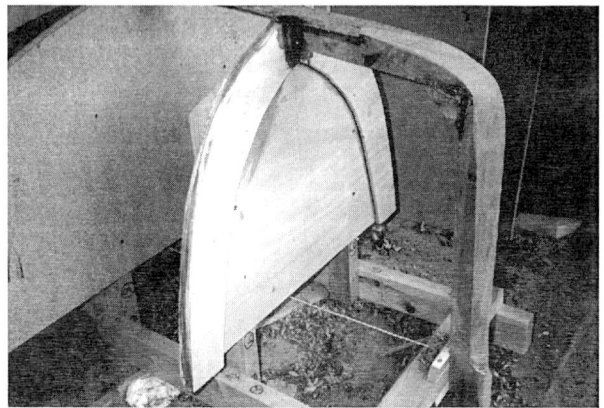

Above—the inner stem of a 13' Woodlark bevelled ready to receive the planking.

The planking must obviously not glue itself to the moulds, but will be glued to the backbone structure. Therefore, the edges of the moulds need to be covered in some way to prevent excess glue from causing problems later. One way to do this is simply to cover the edges of the moulds with masking tape. I then like to rub wax from a candle onto this just to make sure. On canoes you can possibly get away with simply rubbing wax or paraffin onto the mould edge.

5.2 The Lay of the Planking (also refer to Chapter 1)

The way the planks lie over the moulds, and therefore the way they appear in the finished hull, will depend upon the type and shape of hull you are building and on how you want the planking to look, once the hull is complete. Obviously, this latter point will not matter if the strip planking is to be paint finished or covered by veneers.

Most builders like the planking to start at the sheer (gunwale) and to follow the sheer curve so that at least in the portion of the hull above the waterline, the planking appears to lie in a normal sweep similar to that of carvel planking (see Figure 8 for the start of this). On some shapes of hulls and especially those with fine ends and fat midsections, the planking will start to take on a hogged look, because the girth in the middle of the boat is much greater than the girth at the ends. Indeed, with some boats and notably catboat hulls, the curve down in the planking towards the ends of the boat can become too great for the planking to bend round. In this case the planking may need to lie in 2 different directions to overcome this, first being parallel to the sheer line and then the lower part of the hull being planked separately fore and aft (Figure 66 and Figure 11).

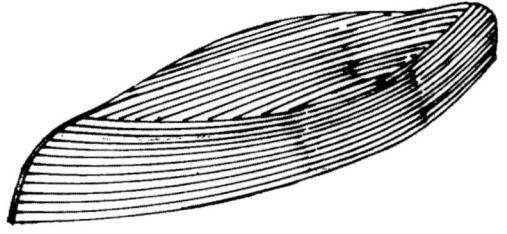

Fig 66. Planking started at the gunwale and stopped when the bend and twist get too much for the planking to lie well against the moulds and started again from the centerline.

Above—the planking started at the gunwale on this Innishmore 10' dinghy built by John Dyson.

Sometimes it is easier to start at the bilge and allow the plank to follow the 'great circle route' over the hull as already mentioned in Chapter 2 and shown in Figure 10. Planking then continues above and below this first plank (Figure 67). The planking in the topsides will sweep up towards the bow and stern which some builders may find ugly. Boats with fantail or counter sterns are best planked this way as the planking needs to lie fore and aft over the stern (Figure 13). It is impossible to bend the planking around the fantail in order to allow it to lie parallel to the sheer. Canoe sterned craft also require the

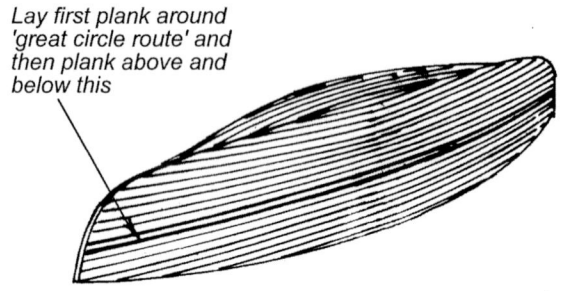

Lay first plank around 'great circle route' and then plank above and below this

Fig 67. Planking started on the 'great circle route' and continued above and below this line.

planking laid this way. In this case, in order to get the planking as parallel to the sheer as possible, position the first plank to go around the 'great circle route' comfortably but with it's mid portion kept as high as possible up the topsides of the hull. Make sure that the lie of the plank is still fair though.

Above—A 21' Skua yacht by Lionel Davis with the planks laid starting on the 'great circle route' showing how the planks run out over the gunwale—but planking overall, is easier.

Where there is a tight curve, perhaps at the turn of the bilge, the plank width can be reduced. A reduction of 10-15% is often enough, but if you are having to order your planks in from a supplier, then it could be a good idea to order, say 12% of them with a 30% reduction in width.

With a Canadian canoe which usually has a high sweeping bow and stern, you will not be able to get the sheer plank to bend to the gunwale line at the ends of the boat. In this case allow the plank to follow the sheer line as far as possible and then allow it to run out over the bow and stern. The portion of hull above this plank at the ends of the canoe can then be planked with short pieces of plank later (Figure 68).

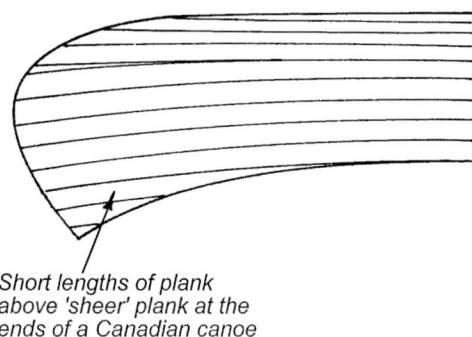

Short lengths of plank above 'sheer' plank at the ends of a Canadian canoe

Fig 68. Planking the swept up bow of a Canadian canoe with short lengths of plank.

5.3 Joining the Plank Lengths

In many cases you will not be able to buy plank stock which is long enough to go round the boat unless you pay a large premium for it. Planks may be butt joined together during the planking process. This is better done, if the planking used is cove/convex edged because this type of planking will hold the 2 pieces of plank together in line. If you do use butt joins in the plank lengths, do make sure that they are well staggered. There should be at least 4' (1220mm) between butts on adjacent planks and butts should not occur within the same frame space (if frames are fitted) unless there are 3 planks between them. Better still, of course, is to scarf the

The Planking Process

plank lengths together. Scarf lengths are usually 8 times the thickness of the plank so that a 1/2'' (12mm) thick plank will use scarf joints which are 4'' (100mm) long (Figure 69).

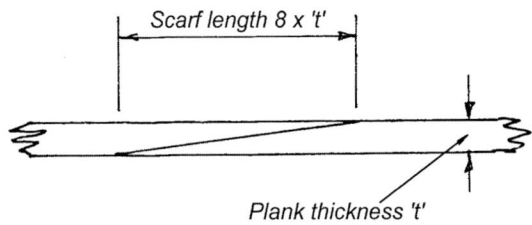

Fig 69. Scarf length.

Scarfs may be cut by hand by clamping the 2 pieces of plank to be joined together on edge (Figure 70). The scarf is then carefully marked on the top plank and very carefully down the sides of the planks. Hold the planks in a vice and then use a back saw (Tenon saw) to carefully cut down the line watching the vertical lines as you go. Start by drawing the saw back on the forward edge of the line across the top plank a couple of times to start the groove. Then saw back and forth making sure that the saw cuts along the top line drawn. Once you have gone down a couple of

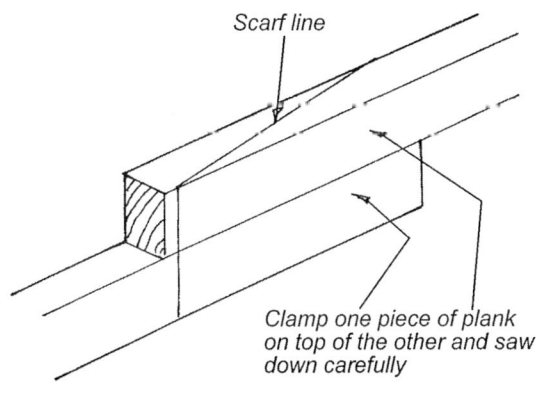

Fig 70. Cutting a scarf join on both pieces of wood at the same time.

millimetres watch the vertical line facing you, as you saw down at an angle. Also, go out and buy a new back saw or at least get your old one well sharpened.

Because so many scarfs are to be cut, a scarfing jig is a good idea. This can be in a form similar to a standard mitre box. Use good flat 1/2'' (12mm) wood stock and screw two uprights to a base. The base should be wide enough to take the plank stock with room for a wedge to hold the plank in place. Make the sides deep enough for the width of the plank plus an inch to guide the saw blade (Figure 71). Having done this, carefully mark the scarf line onto the top and sides of the box. Saw this line very carefully in a similar method to that mentioned for hand cutting the scarf. The plank may be held down in place against the forward side (fence) of the box with cramps or with a wedge.

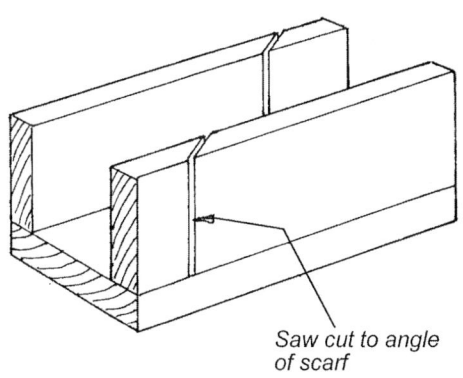

Fig 71. A scarfing box.

In gluing the scarf together, I prefer to use some temporary mechanical fastening to keep the plank pieces in line after the glue has been applied. I very often find, especially when using epoxy glue that the 2 wood pieces tend to slip over each other. Make up a box similar to that used for cutting the scarf but without the front side. Lay one plank piece on it's back with the scarf facing upper most and clamp into place. Position the other plank piece over it and clamp down. Drill for the fastening (I tend to use steel screws) and fasten the two pieces together. If you use two fastenings then the plank will be straight when glued together. If there is only room for one fastening then once the plank has been glued together you will need to use a long straight edge to make sure that the plank pieces are in line with each other.

5.4 Planking

Having established the position of the first plank, pin it to the moulds with nails allowing the head of the nail to remain proud so that it can be removed easily. Staples may also be used. It is a good idea with hulls which are going to be varnish finished over glass sheathing to take care in lining up the nails or staples so that the marks left by the temporary fastenings are in line. If using cove/convex edged planks, the cove (concave) part should be uppermost so that it will act as a gutter for the glue. Carefully check this first plank so that it runs in a fair line and that the plank is equally placed on both sides of the hull.

When screwing planks to chipboard moulds, you may need to use over long screws because of the low holding power of chipboard. For solid wood moulds, the screws should have a length at least twice the thickness of the planking. If you have problems, especially where the plank is under some stress, then screw or glue small wood blocks to the mould and screw through the plank into these (similar to the method shown on Figure 51). The screws should be fitted with large washers under their heads so that the heads do not indent the planking.

Before applying the next plank, you will need to sort out a method for keeping the planks in line with each other, especially if the planking is square edged and therefore not self aligning. On small boats and canoes, simply fastening the planks to the moulds may be enough otherwise, between the moulds you will need to use some form of clamping system first to hold the planks tight against each other and second to hold them in line. A useful tool which is easy to make up is a piece of thick ply or chipboard cut into a 'U' shape. The width of the 'U' should be the same as the thickness of the planking plus a small margin (Figure 72). On larger planking this ply clamp is used in conjunction with wedges against the planks.

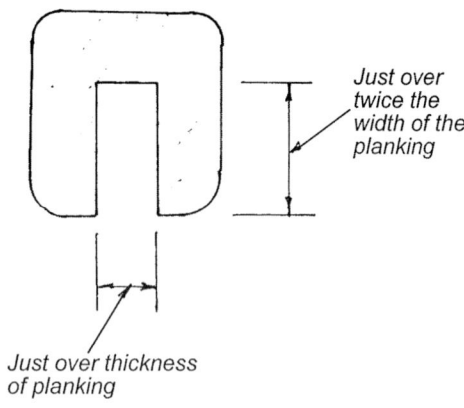

Fig 72. Simple 'U' clamps.

Above—'U' clamps being used on the planking of Derek Hopkins' Woodlark 13' Catboat.

The Planking Process

Another method, is to use thin strips of ply roughly an inch wide which are then nailed up the outside of the hull as each plank goes on. This can be done at the moulds so that the nails here are easy to remove (Figure 73). Where the planks cross the backbone structure they are permanently glued and screwed. Make small adjustments with a plane, on the bevel of the stem, in order to make the planks lie flat with each other. For canoes and small boats, you can use staples in between the moulds, to attach one plank to it's neighbour.

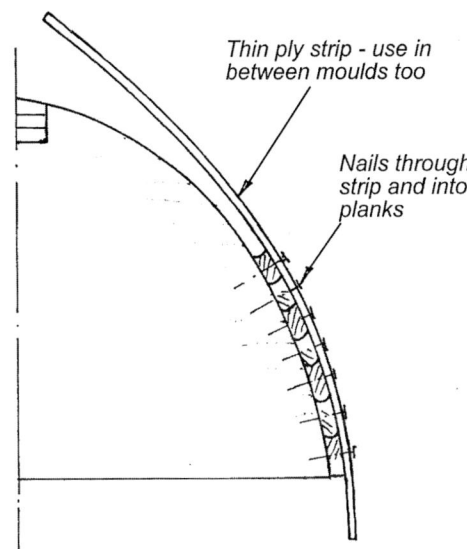

Fig 73. Using strip ply with nails to hold the planks in pace against the moulds.

Offer up the plank, dry, and make a large pencil tick across it and the plank already in place once it is in the right position. Run the glue into the concave (cove) of this first plank and press the second plank into it nailing it to the moulds. If using square edged planks it is often better to apply the glue with a brush or roller to the underside of the next plank rather than the top of the plank already in place. The big rule is to clean off excess glue as you go, both inside and outside the hull. This will greatly aid cleaning the hull up later. Builders develop their own tricks for applying the glue to the plank (rather than to themselves!). The glue can be applied with a brush, but this is often slow and inaccurate, or a device similar to a disposable cake icing bag can be used with a nozzle of big enough size to allow a good bead of glue to be applied. As an alternative, a strong polythene bag with a small amount of it's corner cut off, will work well (Balcotan 100 is applied directly from the bottle). With epoxy, apply some unfilled resin (with hardener mixed) to the plank which is being applied and then the filled (thickened) epoxy to the plank already in place.

Match up the ticks as you position the plank and fasten it at it's centre then skip fore and aft several feet and fasten again and repeat this to the bow and stern. This gets the plank in position quickly, before the glue runs everywhere. Now you can go in between to apply more fastenings. Some builders set themselves up so that they lay several planks together with the edges to be glued uppermost and lightly clamp them together. Then they apply glue over the whole lot. The planks are then released from the clamps as they are needed. If you are working in a team and work fast (before the glue starts to set), this can be a quick and less messy way of applying the glue.

Try to keep the planking even, in numbers both sides of the hull. This will ensure that the hull does not become twisted by having unequal stresses applied during construction. The stem, especially of canoes and small boats, can be twisted out of line if the progress of the planking is not kept equal on both sides. Once a large portion of the planking is complete, keeping the planking equal on both sides, becomes less important and you may find it convenient to work on one side only.

Take particular care to ensure that the planks lie hard up against and in-line, with the neighbouring plank. Use additional fastenings where necessary to achieve this but do not overdo the fastenings where they are not needed. The problem areas to look out for are at the bilge where the planking will want to pull away from it's neighbor as the planking progresses down the bilge towards the hog (Figure 74). Use two fastenings here, one to hold the plank flat to it's neighbor and the other to hold it to the mould. In some craft and depending upon how wide the planking is, you will need to stop at some point because the stress of getting the plank in position and flat, is too great. At this point you will need to change the direction of the planking which will mean cutting the ends of the rest of the planks to lie against the inner edge of the last plank that you were able to sweep around (Figure 66).

Above—planking the bilge towards the hog on the 13' woodlark. Note the double twist in the planking as it goes from the bilge area towards the stem. This is partly eased by the use of thinner planks in this area.

the plank to mark along the underside of the new plank where the planking already in place cuts it (Figure 75). There will be some bevel required on this cut and therefore do not cut directly to the line, but leave an allowance. Mark and cut one end first, bevel it with a block plane and fit the plank in place using clamps or temporary nails. Mark the under side of the other end and remove the plank for the final end to be cut and planed.

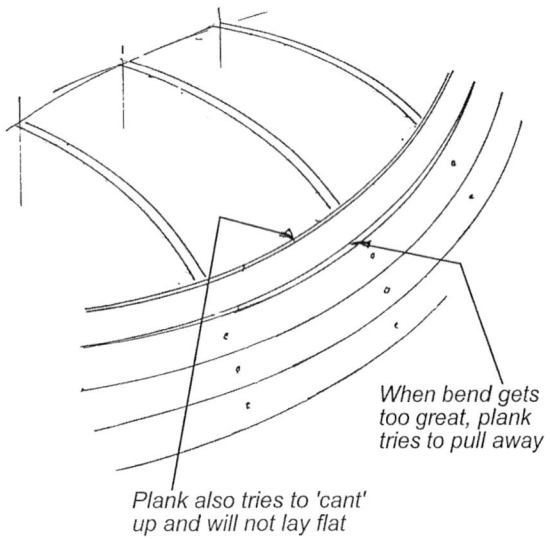

Fig 74. Planking laid from the gunwale tries to 'lift' away from the moulds at the turn of the bilge..

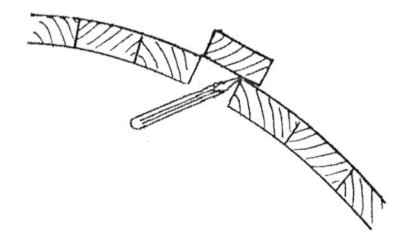

Fig 75. Marking the final plank.

Take care to get a good joint. This can be done by lying the plank over the position it is to take up. Then use a pencil from up under

In canoes and boats with a fairly deep fore foot at the bow, the planking may not want to lie easily in line with it's neighbours as you move down towards the hog. The planking is trying to 'compound' (bend in three directions at once) in this area and you may get to a point where using more fastenings is not holding the planking flat with it's neighbours because it is trying to 'cock up' onto it's inside corner leaving an outside corner proud and the plank not lying flat against the beveled surface of the inner stem (Figure 76). In this case, position the plank with a gap between it and it's neighbour and fit a tapered piece of planking called a 'stealer' or 'cheater' (Figure 77). Depending upon the shape of the hull, these stealer planks may need to be fitted elsewhere. If you are using cove/convex edged planking you will need to plane the mating surfaces flat for a tapered plank.

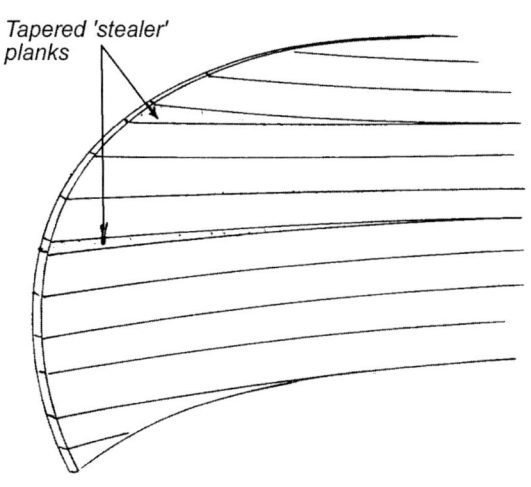

Fig 77. Allowing the planks to lie with a gap which can then be in-filled.

Above—'stealers' and tapered planks on an Edwardian 26.

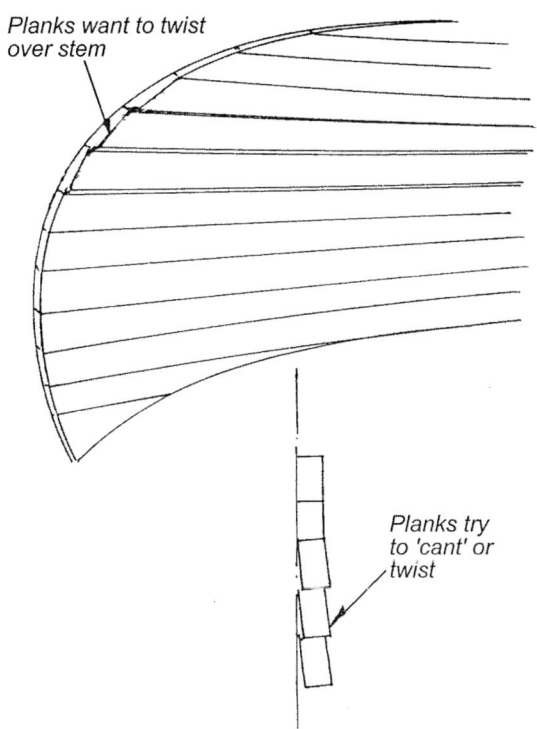

Fig 76. Problems with the planking of a Canadian canoe trying to 'cock up' onto it's corner as it goes over the bow.

How you plank over the hog will very much depend upon the direction in which you have planked. If you have planked parallel to the sheer down to the bilge area and then planked towards the bilge area from the hog, then these latter planks will run naturally parallel to the hog (Figure 66). However, if you have planked from the sheer down all the way, the planks will be running out over the hog. In this case it is often best to plank on both sides down to the end of the stem/beginning of the hog and then to plank over the hog on one side only. Having done this, draw the centreline onto the top of these planks and trim the excess off. You can then plank the other side cutting the ends to fit (Figure 78). On canoes, which have little or no outside stem/keel runner and in hulls which have a very flat sections in the hog area, this way of finishing the planking is essential. The last plank will have to have the outer edge of it's 'cove' removed otherwise you will not be able to slip it into place. Gaining the shape for this last plank can be difficult and may require some trial and error. Laying it over the gap and marking from underneath never seems to work well because there is often too much shape and bevel to deal with. You can certainly do this to start with but do cut initially well outside the line and trim by trial and error from then on.

If the boat has a large outside stem/keel piece which will require a flat area planed onto the planking, to take it, then it is perfectly permissible to plank one side, over the hog and to simply bevel this off, to take the planking on the other side (Figure 79). When using fastenings, remember the flat area that will be planed off for the outer stem/keel and keep fastenings away from this area.

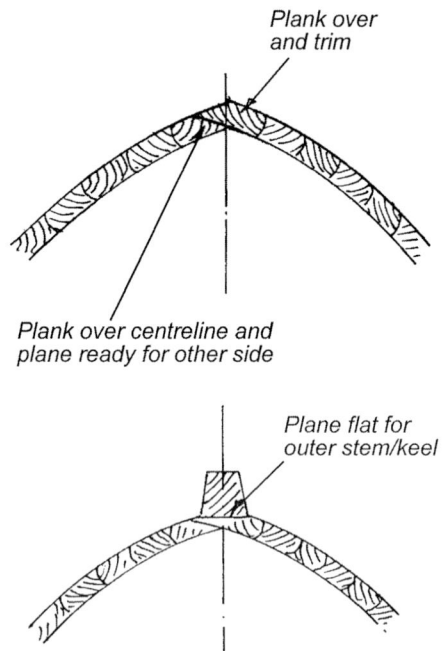

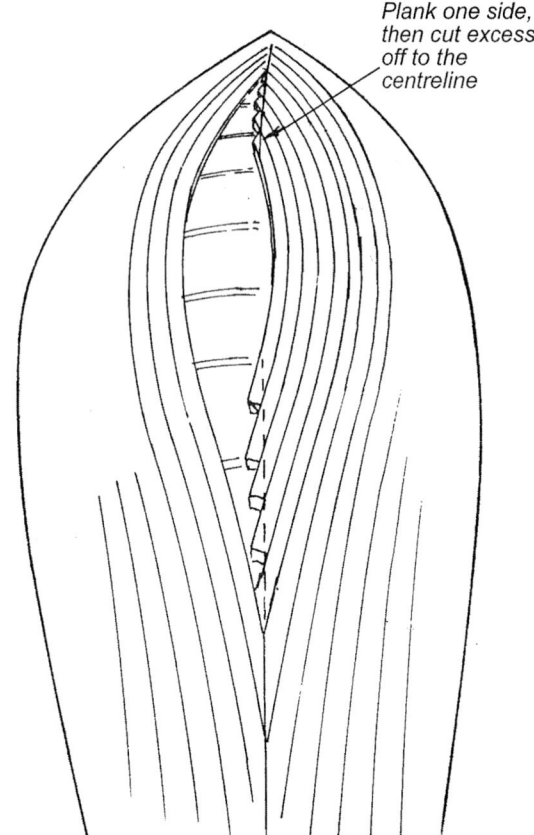

Fig 78. Dealing with the planks as they meet on the centerline of a canoe.

Fig 79. Planking meeting on the centerline of a hull where there is an outside keel or skeg.

The hog being bevelled on the 23'3" Frigate's Boat.

Chapter 6
FINISHING THE HULL

6.1 Cleaning Up the Hull

I cannot emphasize enough the need to 'work clean' and to remove excess glue from both the inside and outside of the hull as you plank. You will curse yourself later if you do not and will inevitably end up sanding off too much of the planking in order to get it clean of epoxy. Why give yourself so much extra work when some fore thought and a little effort in wiping off excess epoxy before it sets, will greatly reduce the amount of work you have to do in cleaning the hull up? As mentioned earlier, when talking about Balcotan 100 glue, if you have used this to glue the planks together, then it is easier to leave the excess to cure and to scrape it off later. But do not be tempted to do this with epoxy.

The first stage in cleaning the outside of the hull up is to remove all the temporary fastenings and all those tying the hull to the jig. Cedar will scratch and bruise easily, so great care needs to be taken in doing this, unless the planking is going to be veneered. For staples, a screw driver with it's tip bent at about 30 degrees will act as a good lifter but do protect the Cedar underneath the bend of the screw driver so that it is not bruised when lifting the staple (Figure 80). If the staples have been inserted over old lighting flex, the flex can be pulled up, which brings one end of the staple out of the wood, allowing you to remove it with a pair of pliers. For nails, try to pull the nail out directly without rotating the pincers against the planking or if you do, put a thin ply pad between the pincer and the plank.

Next, trim all the ends of the planks which over reach the stem, transom etc. Now you can remove any excess epoxy which may be around. Some epoxies will respond to paint remover. Apply this and then let it sit for 15 to 20 minutes. You should then be able to remove the epoxy with a scraper. I do not like using paint strippers myself, so do this with caution and try it on a part of the hull which will not be seen later, first.

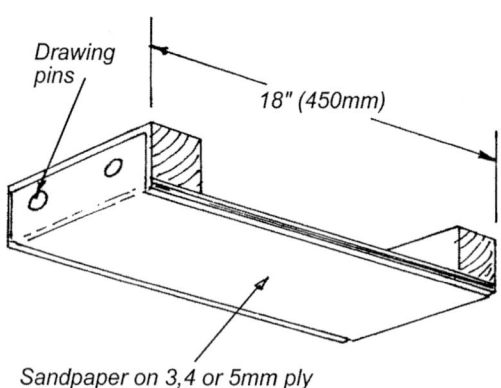

Fig 81. The sanding board.

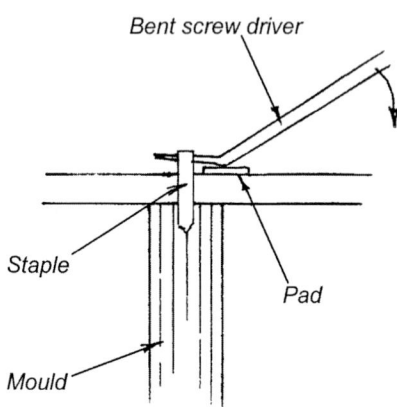

Fig 80. Removing nails and staples without damaging the planking.

Next, the hull surface needs to be sanded. Inevitably there will be some misalignment between some of the planks although, again, it's a case of the more time spent in lining planks up during the planking process, the less time taken in having to sand down irregularities. Remember, Cedar does scratch easily and this will show through even the glass sheathing. Therefore, it is better to do the sanding by hand using long sanding boards. A board around 18'' (450mm) long can be made from 3,4 or 5mm ply (depending on how flexible the board needs to be to suit the curvature of the surface being sanded) with a piece of 1 1/4''x1 1/4'' (30x30) pine at each end (Figure 81). Buy the sandpaper in a roll so that it can be attached to the pieces of pine by drawing pins. Using a long sanding board means that you will not over sand in one small area, but will fair the whole hull. Use something like 50 grit to start with and sand at an angle to the plank lines. Once all irregularities have gone, change the sandpaper for 80 grit and then 120 grit finishing off in the same direction as the planks.

Lightly applying water to the wood surface will show up any scratches which still exist. You will need to go this far, if the Cedar is to be clear varnish finished with a glass cloth sheathing. If the hull is to be veneered, there is no need to go beyond the initial sanding stage.

6.2 Glass Sheathing the Hull

First decide what may need to be added to the hull before sheathing. Rubbing strakes and bilge runners should go on 'over' the sheathing and are therefore put on after the sheathing has been applied. On the other hand, the drawings may specify that the outer stem is put on and sheathed over. Deadwood would normally be put on after the outside sheathing and before the hull is rolled upright. Do not be tempted to sheath up to a rubbing strake as this inevitably leads to a mess and a source where water can later ingress behind the sheathing (Figure 82). Any exterior sheathing should go on after the internal structure has been through fastened to the hull so that all heads of fastenings are covered up. This may cause a problem in that the hull will need to be turned over and removed from the jig whilst the interior structure is fitted and fastened through the hull and then turned back upside down for sheathing. Holes left by fastenings and the heads of permanent fastenings should be filled with thickened epoxy.

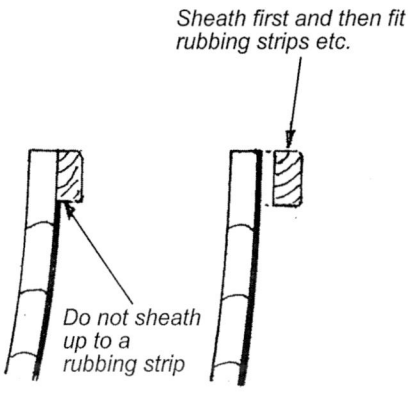

Fig 82. Sheath first and fit rubbing strakes, outer stems etc., later.

Having structurally got the hull to the sheathing stage, great care should be taken in removing any dust and debris as this will show up in the sheathing. Dust the hull down and vacuum both the hull and the workshop.

Next, we want to prepare the glass cloth by pre cutting it to shape. It is handy to have the cloth on what amounts to a long towel rail, so that it can be rolled off as required and you want some form of long wood bar to hang it over once it has been cut. The idea is to distort the cloth as little as possible and folding the cloth or draping it carelessly will inevitably result in it picking up debris and being pulled out of shape. The designer may have specified the lay of the cloths and the overlaps but generally speaking for a canoe or small boat the cloth is laid fore and aft. The cloth may be laid in 2 halves overlapping at the centre of the bottom of the boat (keel) or a piece may be laid centrally over the keel and additional clothes laid over each side.

Larger boats will often have their cloths laid vertically from keel to gunwale with each overlapping the next down the sides. The amount of overlap will vary depending upon the weight of cloth used and the size of boat. For a canoe the overlap along the centreline wants to be around 1 1/2" (36mm) and 1" (25mm) at the stem. For larger boats above 20' in length the overlap should be around 3" (75mm) at the keel and the overlap between the sides of the vertically laid cloth should be 1 1/2" (75mm). This will be dressed off later to make it flat (Figure 83).

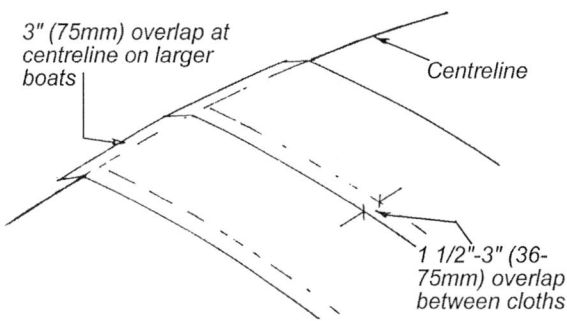

Fig 83. Overlaps in the sheathing.

I normally 'prime' the wood surface with epoxy resin first but I know that some builders do not. I prefer to do this because the wood itself can tend to draw resin away from the cloth. Sealing the wood first with a priming coat of resin prevents this from happening. If, after the priming coat has partially cured, the surface looks dull and matt, then let it cure hard and then sand lightly and coat again. If the surface remains glossy, then you can apply the cloth straight onto the priming resin before it fully cures. If there are any large voids to fill in the surface of the hull, let the resin cure and then fill with a resin putty before proceeding with the sheathing. If the hull is to be clear finished you will need to make the filler look as natural as possible and this can be done by mixing alcohol based stains into the resin.

There are basically two methods for applying the cloth. The 'wet' method and 'dry' method. With the 'wet' method you apply the resin to the wood surface first and then lay the cloth onto it, rolling it down with split washer rollers. The problem here, is that you have to work fast in order to get the whole piece of cloth that you are working on, thoroughly wetted out before the resin starts to cure. This means having a team to help you. If you are working on vertical surfaces, this is really the easier way to do it. Use the slow hardener for the 'wet' method.

The 'dry' method entails holding the cloth into position with some tape, and then working resin into the cloth from above ensuring that it becomes well wetted out with no dry areas. This method is easier, in that, it allows you to work at your own pace without having to rush in order to wet the cloth out before all the previously applied resin cures but it is difficult to use it on vertical surfaces and you must ensure a thorough wetting out of the cloth and the removal of all air bubbles.

Work from the centre of the cloth in both cases using split washer rollers, foam covered rollers or squeegees (thin plastic). If you use a sqeegee, pour some resin onto the surface and then hold the sqeegee at approximately 75 degrees and apply light but firm pressure as you move the resin about. Do not over work an area especially with epoxy as this will tend to create bubbles in the resin. Mix up around a quart of resin in a large yogurt pot and pour this into a tray so that it is spread out. Epoxy left in a mixing container will cure quickly because of the bulk heat reaction. Spreading the epoxy out slows this process down.

Changes in shape in the surface being sheathed ie., from curve to flat will mean that the cloth will need to be cut, as it is not possible to loose cloth by folding it. Consequently, darts will need to be cut out and the edges overlapped. The overlaps should be well rolled down which will make them almost disappear. On smaller boats, if you are wanting to finish with an absolutely perfect surface which shows off the underlying wood grain, then the edges of the cloth can butt against each other leaving a flush surface. To do this, overlap the cloths slightly, and when the resin has partially cured, use a scalpel to cut a line through both cloths. The piece of cloth underneath can then be removed along with the excess piece on the top and the two cloths smoothed down exactly butting each other.

Whilst applying the glass cloth, use just enough resin to fully wet out the cloth and do not overload the surface with resin or you will get runs. Once all the glass cloth has been applied, allow it to cure for 48 hours and then sand off any pieces of cloth sticking up. Sand the entire hull with a medium grit sandpaper and then coat with epoxy, again looking out for runs. Any external structure can now be applied ie. rubbing strakes, deadwood, runners etc. In fact, you may wish to leave the rubbing strakes until the hull is turned over so that you can finally establish and fair in the sheer line with the boat upright. Minuscule amounts of error in the line of the sheer can throw the look of the whole boat out and you cannot gauge this with the hull upside down.

Use a rasp to flatten the surfaces where any exterior structure is to go. External stems can often be laminated in situ although there may be a difficulty in holding the laminations down. In this case take a pattern off the hull for the 'inner' shape of the stem and laminate the outer stem in much the same way as the inner stem. The shapes of skegs and deadwood can be taken from the hull using hardboard templates and then these items can be fitted to the hull. Any large components can be epoxied to the hull and then have holes drilled for bolts or they can be screwed up through from inside the hull. The epoxy glue will make sure that they do not move. All corners between the hull and these external components should be filled with epoxy filleting.

The entire hull now wants to be sanded and again the best tool for this is the long board with 50 grit sandpaper. Take the time to remove irregularities and to get the hull smooth all over. Obviously, do not go through the glass cloth but finish with 80 grit paper before applying a final coat of epoxy resin to the entire hull.

6.3 Veneering the Hull

If the exterior of the hull is to be veneered, then what we have described for the glass sheathing will still apply, but after the veneers have been secured to the hull. Normally the veneers are put onto the hull diagonally, at approximately 45 degrees. Two layers are often used with the first layer lying at 45 degrees aft and the outer layer laying at 45 degrees forward (or visa versa). Hence the layers of veneers lie at 90 degrees to each other (Figure 84). Sometimes the outer veneer is positioned fore and aft to emulate normal carvel planking.

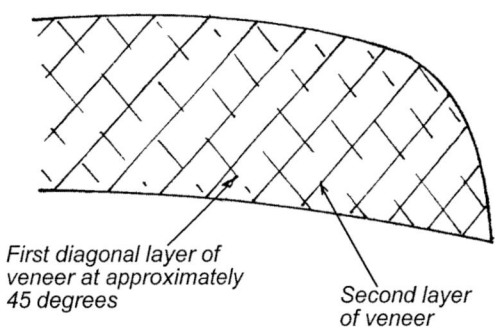

First diagonal layer of veneer at approximately 45 degrees

Second layer of veneer

Fig 84. Applying the veneers diagonally.

The width of the veneer planks will depend upon the width of veneers bought in and on the amount of compound curvature that the hull has. It may also depend upon the aesthetics (looks) that you want to achieve in that some builders do not like the look of wide planking. If the hull has a lot of compound curvature (for instance a hull which is wide amidships with narrow ends) then in order to cope with the compound curve, the planks will need to be fairly narrow. A long lean hull (ie. a traditional steam launch) may have little compound curvature in it's shape and therefore the planks could be wider. You will want to get the most out of whatever width of veneer you have bought and if the veneer averages out at around 10" (250mm) wide then the planks that you will be able to get out of it may have a maximum width of 4 1/2" (115mm). You will soon see if the plank width is too wide, because the edges of the veneer will be difficult to hold down due to the compounding that the veneer is trying to do.

Most veneers are applied in 2 to 3mm thicknesses and in calculating the amount of veneer required you will have to allow for around 25% for wastage. The short pieces cut off from the ends of the veneer planks are almost all useless and cannot be used elsewhere on the hull. It is perfectly acceptable to butt join veneers or even to scarf them which will help cut down wastage. Joins in the plank lengths may be done on the hull and they should be staggered (Figure 85).

Above—the final layer of diagonal veneer added to Giuseppe Casalino's 18' Tosher.

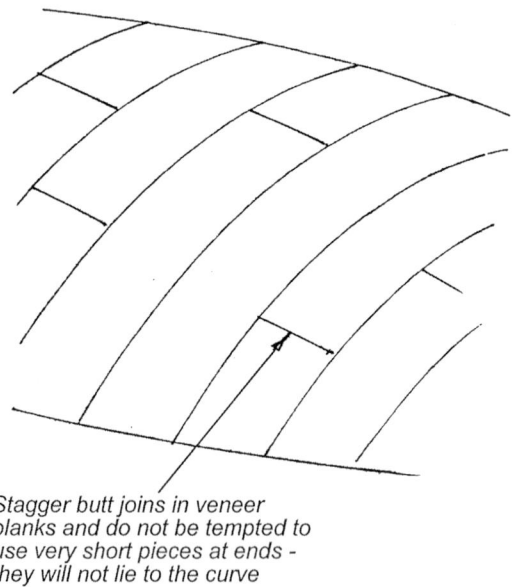

Stagger butt joins in veneer planks and do not be tempted to use very short pieces at ends - they will not lie to the curve

Fig 85. Arranging the butts in the veneers.

The first job, after you have taken delivery of the veneers, is to grade them for quality and colour. The lower grade veneers should be used on the inner layer and you can arrange the colours to suit your own requirements. Some builders like to have a good assortment of colour spread throughout the hull, whilst others like to gradually grade the colours from one end of the boat to the other. Before veneering the hull, it is very important to remove all fastenings tying it to the building jig. Once covered with the veneer you will not be able to get at any through fastenings again.

Having graded the veneers, the next job is to decide on the lay of the first, or master plank. After deciding upon it's width, the plank can be cut from the veneer by first using a long straight edge to mark it out and then a band saw or fine toothed back saw to cut it out. The edges need to be very straight and any bumps may be removed with a small block plane. The plank is placed at the midships position on the hull so that you can work fore and aft of it. Also, it's angle is quite important. If the veneer is placed at too vertical an angle, the veneer may be too stiff to bend without it breaking and if it's angle is too shallow (in other words closer to the horizontal) the effects of the compound hull curve will be greater (Figure 86). Usually, the best angle is 45 degrees but this should be

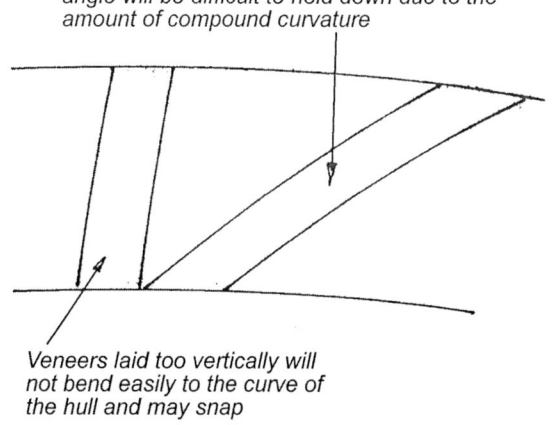

The edges of veneers laid at too shallow an angle will be difficult to hold down due to the amount of compound curvature

Veneers laid too vertically will not bend easily to the curve of the hull and may snap

Fig 86. Deciding the angle of the veneers.

tried on the boat. Having established the correct position the master plank can be glued and fastened to the hull.

The glue may be resorcinal, epoxy or Balcotan 100. If using epoxy, it should be thickened to a ketchup consistency with microfibres or microspheres filler. The epoxy resin by itself does not have enough gap filling ability to fill any voids which may occur. Balcotan 100 expands anyway to fill possible voids. No matter which glue you use, make up a thin plastic sqeegee. This may be a thin piece of plastic measuring 5"x3" (125x75mm) with 1/4" (6mm) serrations cut into the bottom edge. I find it easier to apply the glue to the hull surface, but apart from when using Balcotan some glue should be applied to the veneer to make sure that there are no voids. Pour the glue out onto the surface and then move it over the entire surface with the sqeegee. For 3mm veneer, use 9mm long wide crown staples. These can be left in permanently if they are bronze or aluminium. If they are to be removed, then staple over wire flex or plastic packaging (banding) tape. You will need to staple in rows at 1 1/2" to 2" (36 to 50mm) centres or less, if the curvature of the hull is small and the veneer is thin (Figure 87). Funnily enough, thick veneer applied to a tight curve usually requires fewer staples to hold it down without any voids. You can lightly knock the veneer with a pin hammer to hear whether there are any voids between the veneer plank and the hull. Let the master plank overlap the gunwale and hog.

Because of the curvature of the hull, the next and subsequent planks will need to be 'spiled', to shape them to the edge of the plank already attached to the hull. You can imagine, that, for the edge of the plank you are fitting, to remain straight and to fit against the master plank, the hull would have to have

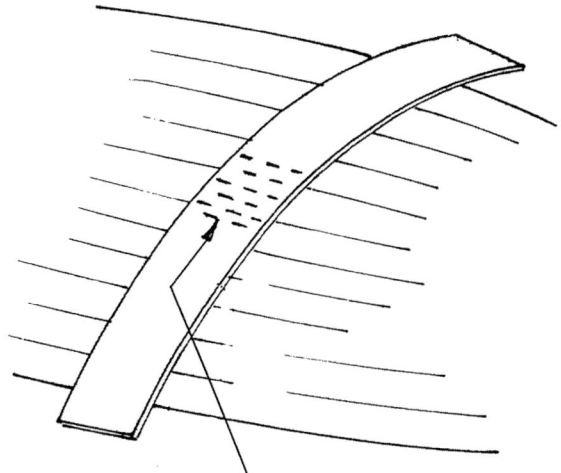

Staple from the centre of the plank out and take particular care to make sure that the edges are well stapled down

Fig 87. Stapling the veneers.

Above—on this 20' Cambrian steam launch by John MacMillan the bottom of the hull below the waterline has been diagonally veneered for additional strength.

a hull shape which had exactly the same section all along it's length. This is obviously not the case though, and so that the planking lies flat to the hull shape, the edge of the next plank has to have some shape in it.

Gaining this shape is not very difficult. All you do is to lightly staple the new plank onto the hull with it's edge touching the edge of the master plank. To lie flat against the hull surface it will only touch the edge of the master plank at it's top and bottom leaving a gap which increases towards the centre of the plank. Take a pair of dividers or compasses and set them to the maximum gap between the two planks. With one point of the dividers/compasses against the edge of the master plank mark this gap width all along the top surface of the plank being fitted (Figure 88). Remove the plank and use a block plane to remove the excess material along the edge of the plank. If there is a lot of material to remove, take most of it off with a band saw. Refit the plank holding it down with some helping hands to check that it is lying flat against the hull surface with no gap between it and the master plank.

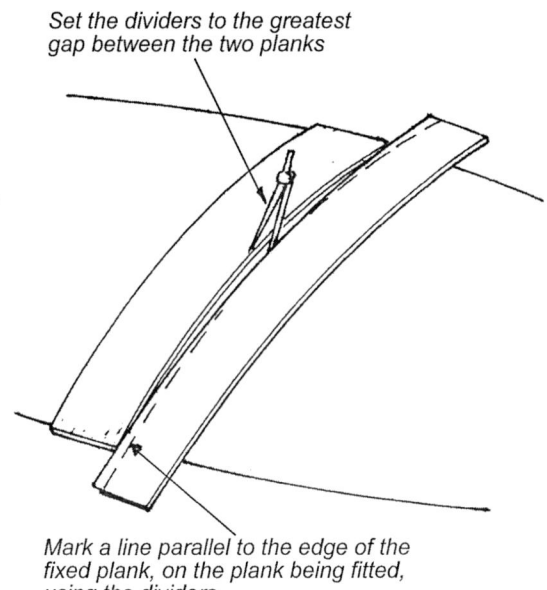

Fig 88. Gaining the shapes of adjacent veneers.

Do not be tempted to glue it into position unless it lies flat naturally without much force, or you will end up with voids below it. In positioning and shaping the planks, do so, in such a fashion, that you remove roughly the same amount of material from the edge of the top and bottom. If you remove more from one end, the angle of the planking will change. Continue this process working fore and aft of the master plank until the whole hull is covered.

The second layer goes on in much the same way except that it lies at 90 degrees to the first layer, but again start at the middle of the hull. Once complete, trim off the excess lengths of plank and fit the outer stem, keel and deadwood. Staples used on the outside veneer are removed, so that they can be steel. Mahogany veneered hulls are not always glass sheathed but if your hull is to be sheathed follow the method described in section 6.2.

The veneers can of course be applied fore and aft. This is often done to simulate traditional planking. Fore and aft veneers do not offer the same cross grain/plank strength that diagonal veneers do and they are often applied over two layers of veneers placed diagonally on cold moulded hulls.

Apart from using mechanical fastenings to hold the veneers in place, some builders vacuum bag the hull so that stables etc do not need to be used but this is not a method easily available to the amateur boat builder. With vacuum bagging, the glue is applied, the veneers are held in place at their ends with fastenings and then the hull shell is inserted into a large tough bag of polythene type material. The air is then removed from the bag by a vacuum pump so that the bag collapses onto the veneer applying a high even pressure over the veneers.

Instead of using solid wood veneers, some builders use plywood. This is partly because plywood is often easier to get hold of and it is usually cheaper. It also tends to be more stable and less prone to wrinkling because at least one of the veneers that go to make up

Finishing the Hull

Above—on this strip planked version of the Kari 3 by Aquiles Rosner the outer veneer has been laid fore and aft to simulate traditional carvel planking.

the plywood is at 90 degrees to the length of the plywood plank. Marine plywood should be used, as opposed to any other grade. It may be more difficult to cut and plane good crisp edges to the sides of the plywood plank.

6.4 The Interior of the Hull

Once the outside of the hull has been finished it needs to be removed from the building jig and turned over. First you want some form of cradle for the hull to sit in once it is up the right way. This can be made up in the form of a couple of female sectional shapes taken from the plans allowing for plank width and some extra for carpeting fastened to the edges of the sectional shapes to protect the hull surface. These sectional shapes want to be tied together on a bed frame set at a convenient height for working on the hull and for fitting the keel and rudder (Figure 89). The secret here is to carefully think through the remainder of the building process. Do you want to have to dig a pit so that you can fit the rudder and stock up into the hull, etc? Some builders find it easier to roll the hull with the jig over and then to extract the jig by means of a lifting tackle but this may make the rolling process too heavy, in which case the hull will need to be lifted vertically from the jig first.

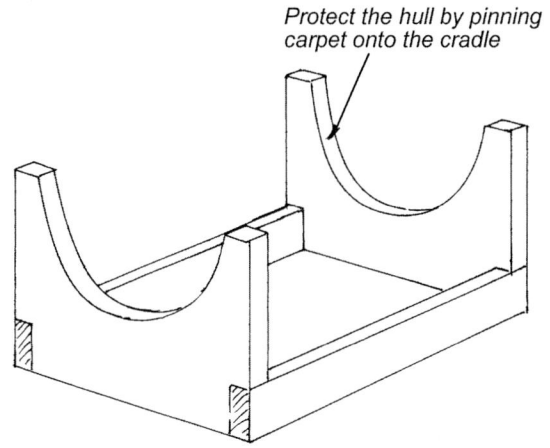

Fig 89. A simple cradle to hold the hull.

Canoes and small boats will not produce problems from the weight point of view and can be released directly from the jig. Larger hulls will require some form of attachment for the lifting tackle. This may be via holes drilled through the hog which will eventually be used for the keel bolts. Before removing the jig, clamber inside the hull and mark on the inside of the hull at each mould the position of the sheer line. This is already marked on each mould and simply needs to be transferred to the inside of the planking.

Once the hull is over and sitting correctly, work can begin on the interior. This is very often sheathed, in which case, the same cleaning up routine will need to be followed, as that use on the exterior of the hull. Because you are now working on a concave surface, the process is more difficult, especially when trying to use planes. Scrapers with slightly rounded blades are good in this situation, but there is still no substitute for cleaning off excess glue during the planking process to give you a flying start.

If plywood bulkheads have been used as some of the moulds in the building jig and the inside of the hull is to be sheathed, these should not have been permanently attached to the planking. Trying to sheath on the inside of the hull, in between the bulkheads, is very difficult and results in a structural break in the sheathing. Sheath first and then refit the bulkheads over the top of the sheathing. This should be done before the inwales (inner gunwale) are fastened into position and a cut out should be made in the bulkhead to accommodate the inwale before the bulkhead is finally fastened in place. Take time to position the bulkheads accurately making sure that they are vertical. To make sure that the bulkheads are square across the boat, use a similar method to that shown in Figure 38 by using diagonal dimensions, at first from the bow to either side of the first bulkhead and then from opposing corners between the subsequent bulkheads.

Before doing anything structural to the interior or before sheathing it, the sheer line wants to be finalised. Having marked on the interior of the hull, the position of the sheer line at each mould position, these points can be joined up with a thin wood batten clamped in place to a smooth fair curve. I find it easier to do this on the outside of the hull, so the marks need to be transferred to the outside either by measurement or by drilling a small hole through, making sure that the drill is horizontal. Spend time checking the sheer line across the boat to make sure both sides are equal. It can be helpful to temporarily refit any bulkheads whilst doing this. Use a straight edge and level gauge to level across from one side of the hull to the other.

6.5 Internal Structure

As we have already mentioned, any internal structure which is fastened through the hull should be fitted before the outside is sheathed, so that the sheathing covers any fastenings. Frames are very often laminated in situ if they are quite small and they may be bonded with epoxy fillets. The same applies to bulkheads, which do not require a wood cleat to fasten them to the hull. They can be bonded with large epoxy fillets perhaps overlaid with glass cloth in bigger boats (Figure 90). Conventional wood filleting may still be used but this will need to be shaped to the hull and glued with epoxy. If the hull has a lot of small laminated or bent frames, the inwale is very often fastened over the top of them trapping them between the inside of the hull and the outboard side of the inwale (Figure 56). If the hull does not have such frames, or only has a few frames then the frames are stopped under the inwale which is attached and glued directly to the inside of the hull.

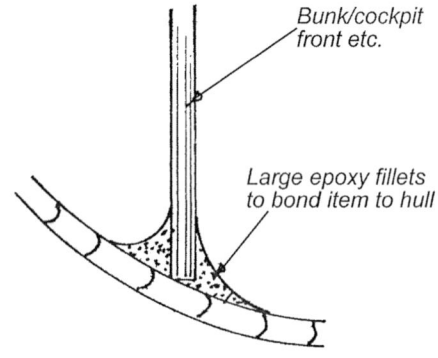

Fig 90. Bonding plywood bulkheads etc to the interior of the hull.

I still like to fit bilge stringers, especially if the craft is a steam launch or one that is going to be trailed, and like the inwale, this can be fitted over any frames if there are enough of them, or directly to the inside of the hull surface in a bed of thickened epoxy. The hull planking should still be fastened to the bilge stringer in either case and this needs to be done before the exterior of the hull is sheathed.

Floors may have been incorporated into the jig as mentioned previously, but if not they should also be fitted and fastened through the hull before it is externally sheathed. This is why fitting them as built up floors in the mould structure is a good idea.

The remainder of the fit out may now proceed. The fitting and fastening of locker fronts, bunk fronts etc to the hull can be regarded in the same way as bonding these items into a fibreglass hull. In the plastic hull you would not attach these items by screwing a wood fillet through the hull to attach the bunk fronts etc to. You would bond them in using glass fibre fillets made up from resin and chopped strand mat. Similarly, such items can be bonded into the strip planked hull with epoxy fillets.

Above—the 13' Woodlark catboat being fitted out with laminated frames, bulkheads and deck structure. The frames have been laminated directly into the hull.

Right—a bow picture of Wash Kohnke's 28'6" Corn Bunting steam launch showing the bilge stringers laminated into slots cut into the moulds before the planking is applied. Fitting the bilge stringer at this early stage is much easier than trying to laminated it later when the hull is turned over for a design which does not use individual laminated frames and uses plywood floors and bulkheads for it's athwartships strength.

Above—a view of the Kari 3 showing it's cedar planking having been applied on the 'great circle route' and fore and aft veneers on the outside—the centreboard case can just be seen, having been fitted against a mould before planking started.

Left—Mike Bell's Edwardian launch showing the bilge stringers laminated after the hull has been turned over on top of the frames. The floors were made up beside the moulds and fitted before the planking. The inwale (beam clamp) is fitted over the frames too.

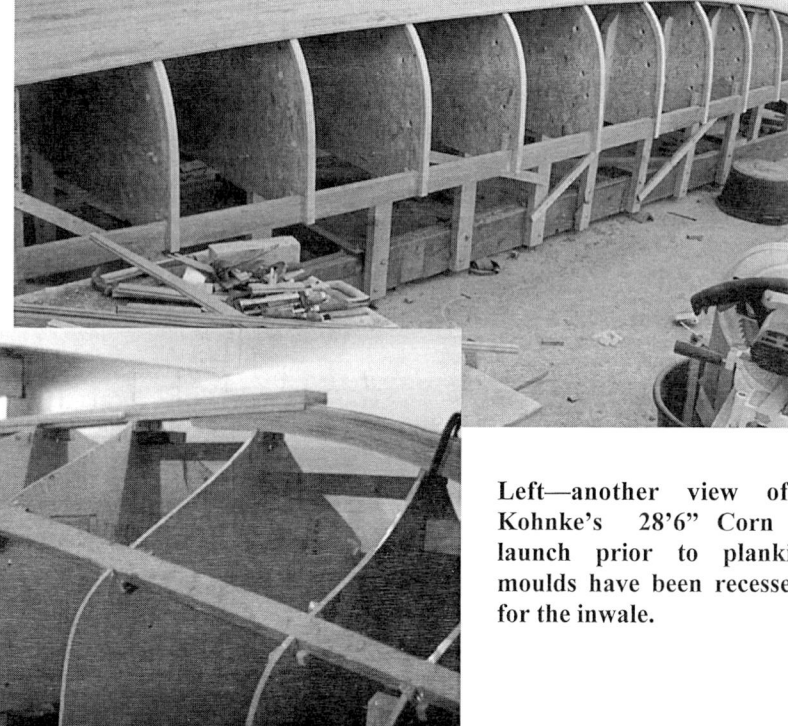

Right—another view of Mike Bell's Edwardian launch "Annabelle" during the planking process—the frames were laminated directly onto the edges of the moulds Herreshoff fashion—the planking is taking the 'great circle route'. Although an easier way to fit the frames (rather than doing it later when the hull has been turned over), this makes the interior of the hull more difficult to clean up.

Left—another view of Wash Kohnke's 28'6" Corn Bunting launch prior to planking—the moulds have been recessed ready for the inwale.

Chapter 7
THE HULL EXTERIOR
KEELS & SKEGS ETC.

7.1 Fitting Gunwale Rubbers etc.

If gunwale rubbers etc are to be replaceable then they can be applied with a layer of mastic (ie., One part 'Life-Caulk' etc) and screwed into place. If they are not designed to be removed then they can be fitted with thickened epoxy and screwed or bolted into place (Figure 91). Note how the lower rubber is fitted to the hull skin only and therefore is screwed into from the hull side—do not try and hold any item onto hull by screwing through the item and into the Cedar strip—it will rarely hold unless the Cedar is massively thick.

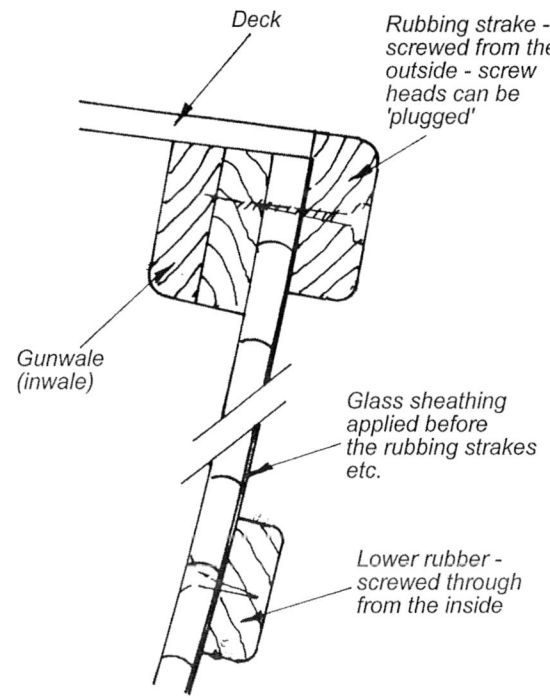

Fig 91. Fitting the rubbing strakes.

7.2 Skegs, Deadwood and Wood Keels

This section covers simple skegs, exterior stems etc and does not touch on ballast keels, fitting sterngear (shafts and stern tubes) or rudders—the construction and fitting of these items is covered in the Selway Fisher Manual of Boat Fit-Out for Yachts and Launches.

If the hull has been built upside down, first consider whether you want to fit the skeg/deadwood permanently before turning the hull upright – bilge keels and central keels can make turning the boat over more difficult and sometimes it is better the make up, shape and fit these items 'dry' before turning the hull over, remove them and finally refit, with the hull upright.

For keel/deadwood and skegs I take a pattern off the hull using scrap wood or hardboard. I shape the edge of the hardboard or scrap wood to exactly fit the area of hull to which the skeg or deadwood/keel is going to be fitted (Figure 92).

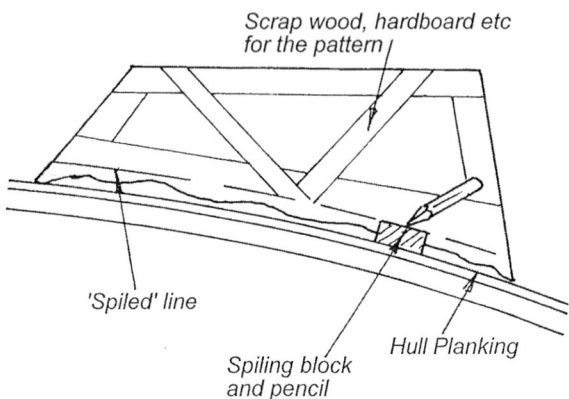

Fig 92. 'Spiling' the shape of the deadwood/skeg off the hull.

I then hold the hardboard in place and, using the Reference/Datum line to take vertical measurements from, draw on the outer shape of the skeg/keel etc. This is then cut to shape and offered back up to the hull for a final check. Any stern-tube or shaft line can be drawn on at the same time. This pattern is then used 'off' the boat to help laminate up the necessary wood or fabricate any steel plate keel etc.

The real item can then be offered up to the hull and taken off for any adjustments to be made before being finally shaped with any tapers etc. Holes for fixing bolts can be drilled and the whole item dry bolted in place.

7.2.1 Fitting Skegs/Deadwood

Figure 93 shows a simple arrangement for a wood skeg on a cruiser. This consists of a wood triangular shaped skeg/deadwood deeper at it's aft end to protect the leg of the outboard or the propeller of an inboard engine. The skeg tapers in it's profile shape towards the bow where it finally blends into the outer stem.

Rather than trying to make up the skeg from one solid piece of wood, it is made up from several horizontal 'lifts' which are glued and bolted together. A solid bottom piece is used to cover the end grain of the horizontal pieces and it is this piece which blends into the outer stem at it's forward end.

To cover the end grain of the 'lifts' at their aft end, a vertical piece may be used which is part 'checked' into the bottom skeg piece.

If the skeg/deadwood is to be bolted it is best to use full length bolts with their bottom ends 'pocketed' into the bottom skeg piece.

The Hull Exterior

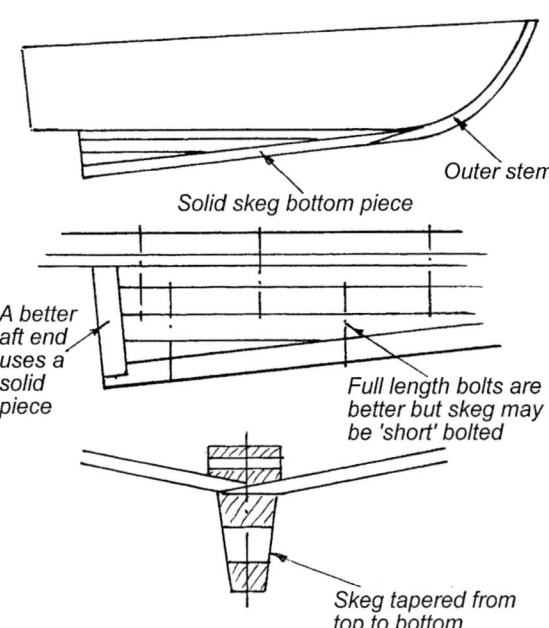

Fig 93. A typical simple triangular skeg/deadwood used on a motor cruiser.

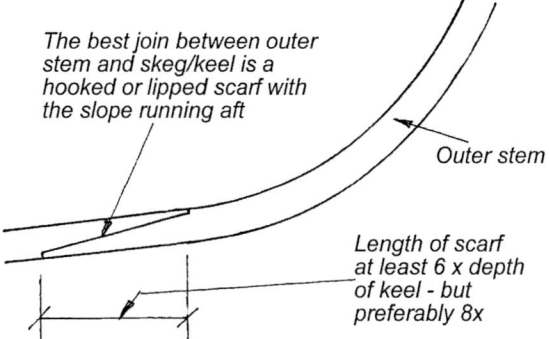

Fig 94. The stem/skeg join.

7.3 The Outer Stem

If we assume that the bow is curved in profile, then the outer stem is usually laminated rather than made up from solid wood pieces. The ends of the Cedar planking need to be planed first, to give a 'flat' area wide enough to take the outer stem. The hull is then usually sheathed at this point before the outer stem, skeg etc is fitted—Figure 95.

However, full length bolts can be difficult to obtain or are expensive and therefore I sometimes use 'short' bolting' - shorter bolts used between the 'lifts' and staggered so that the skeg is adequately fastened.

It is a good idea to use large washers under the bolt heads even though there may not be a lot of stress on the keel—and use large washers under the nuts too. Notice in the section of the skeg shown in Figure 93 that the skeg is usually tapered in section from top to bottom—how much, is usually specified on the drawings. The bottom of the skeg and outer face of the outer stem may also have a bronze or stainless steel covering plate to further protect it.

Where the solid skeg bottom piece joins the outer stem there needs to be a strong and well cut join. This is usually a scarf join (a lipped or hooked scarf is best) with it's slope running aft to protect the skeg should the boat hit something under the water—Figure 94.

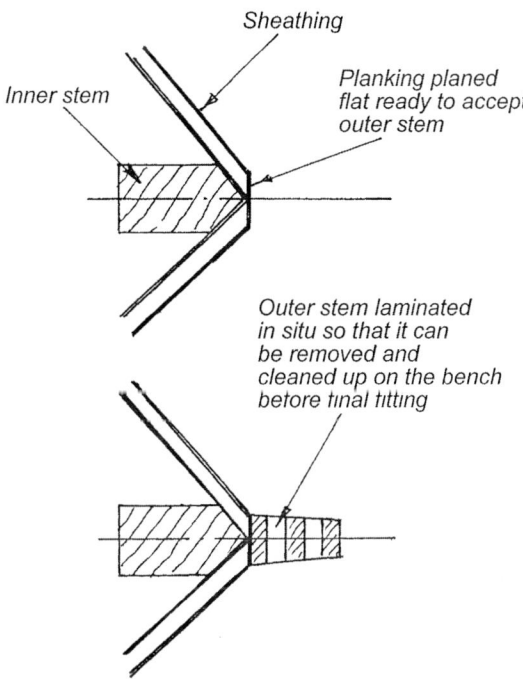

Fig 95. Preparing the hull for the outer stem.

It is difficult to properly clean up and taper the sides of the outer stem when it is fastened to the hull and so I prefer to laminate it in such a way that it can removed and taken to the bench so that it can be finally shaped before final fitting. To do this cover the hull in way of the outer stem with PVC so that glue squeezing from the laminates does not glue the outer stem prematurely to the hull.

To hold the laminates in place I sometimes use timber and wedges braced against the roof of the building shed or dry screw the laminates at their extreme ends so that the screws can be easily removed. Alternatively, you can use screws just long enough to fasten into the adjacent laminates without going right through into the hull.

Once cleaned up, the outer stem can then be refitted with epoxy, to the hull and finally fastened though to the inner stem—Figure 96.

7.4 Bilge Runners

Often, a hull is protected in it's bilge area with fairly small runners (not proper bilge keels). These runners often help to distribute the point loads imposed by bilge rollers on road trailers. The runners are usually tapered top to bottom and at their ends in much the same way as the skeg and can be laminated and fitted in much the same way as the outer stem—Figure 97. It is important to carefully shape and taper the forward and aft ends of the runners so that they create as little turbulence as possible—for a typical runner, say 12' (3.66m) long the tapers should start around 2' (0.61m) from the ends. The ends do not go right down to a point but typically end up 50% of the width and depth of the largest section of the runner.

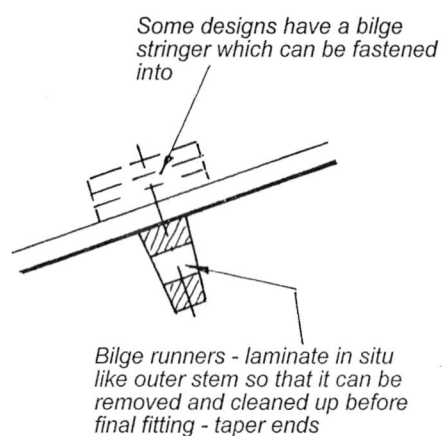

Fig 97. Laminated bilge runners.

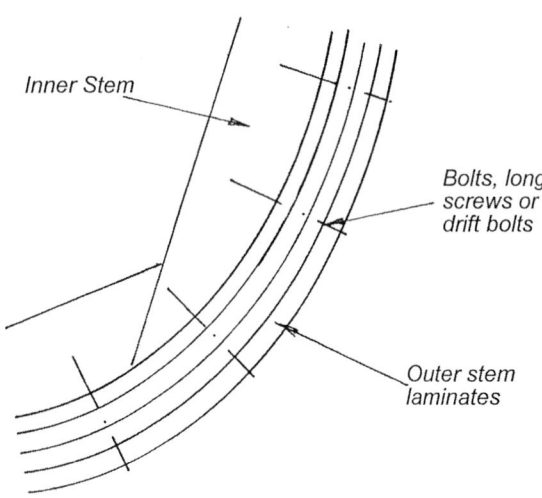

Fig 96. Finally fitting the outer stem to the hull.

Chapter 8
DECK STRUCTURE
SUPERSTRUCTURE & DECK JOINERY

8.1 Decking

8.1.1 The Deck Structure

We will assume that the tops of the athwartship (side to side) plywood frames/bulkheads and fore and aft plywood girders have been cut over height leaving material to be trimmed. For the main deck there are 2 important items to consider – the position of the carlin which defines the plan shape of the coachhouse coaming and the shape of the beams (Figure 98).

I normally start by establishing the position and shape of all of the full beams and then work forward and aft of these for the remaining deck structure. If the deck is to be flat and have no camber, then life is simple and your main complete beam just forward of the coachhouse can be positioned and simply housed into the inwales (Figure 99).

Most yachts have cambered decks, partly for strength and stiffness and also to help shed water off the deck. Establishing the camber curve and therefore the amount of curve for each beam is not too difficult once the camber curve has been established. Each boatyard would have a different way of drawing the camber curve some quite complicated. The problem is, that as well as the width of beam changing as you go forward and aft on the hull, the sheer curve (side profile of the gunwale) changes too. Some builders have quite involved ways of dealing with this but, frankly, so long as you are willing to make small individual adjustments to the curve of the beams, judiciously using a plane, I stick with a fairly simple method.

Deck Structure

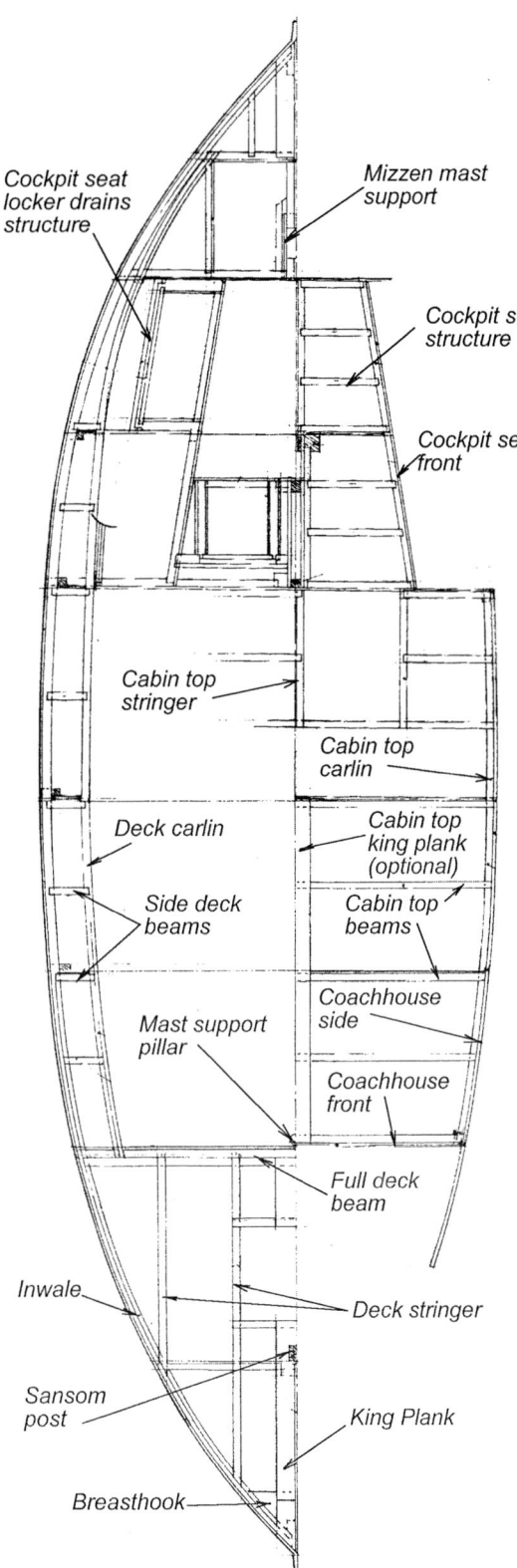

Fig 98. The deck construction plan for the Kari 4—25'1' (7.65m) double ended cruising yacht.

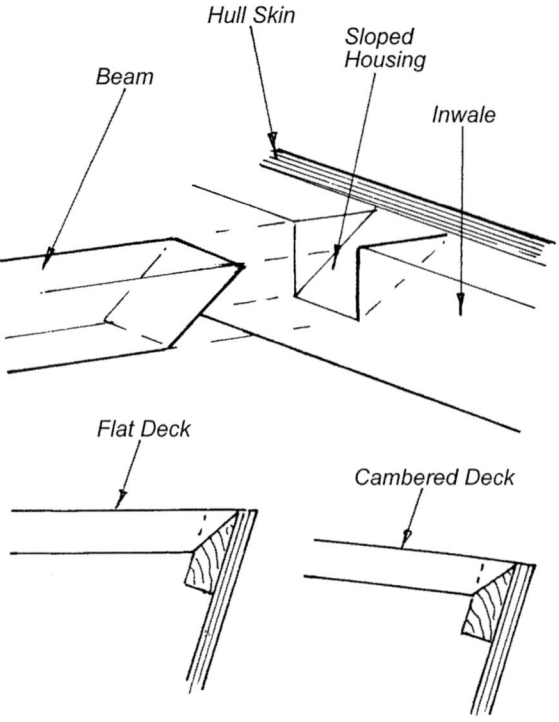

Fig 99. Housing a deck beam into the gunwale for a deck without camber.

First a plywood or scrap wood template is made of the full camber curve. The camber should be marked on the deck construction drawing. Typically for a 24' (7.32m) long boat it will be something like 2 3/4" (70mm in 8' (2.44m) of beam. This means that the maximum depth of the camber (the height of the camber hill, so to speak) is 2 3/4" at a maximum hull beam of 8' – the actual beam of the boat may be slightly less than 8' but this does not matter. As the camber goes forward and the beam reduces, so the camber height reduces until right at the tip of the bow, where there is no beam, there is also no camber.

To make up the template for the camber curve draw a straight line on your template material and at it's centre point raise a perpendicular line. Where these two lines meet use this as the centre of a semi-circle with a radius equal to the maximum camber

Deck Structure

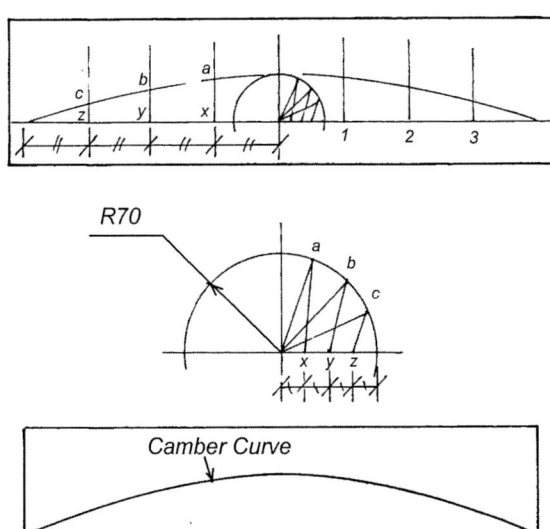

Fig 100. Drawing the camber curve and making a template.

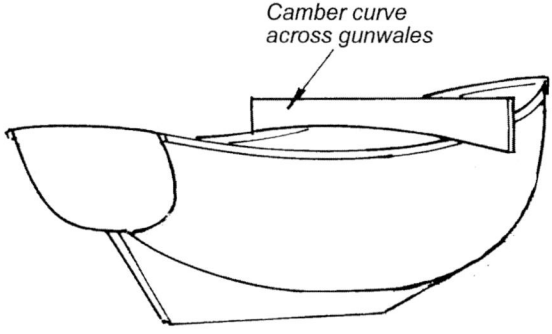

Fig 101. Using the camber curve along the length of the boat.

height. For the length of the horizontal line left and right of this centre mark off your 4' (1/2 beam) and divide these distances into 4 equal parts and raise perpendicular lines (1,2 and 3) at these points.

From the centre of the semi-circle draw lines at 45, 22 ½ and 67 ½ degrees to cut the circle at points a,b and c. Divide the horizontal radius of the circle into 4 equal parts marked x,y and z. the length of the lines x-a, y-b and z-c are then transferred to the lines 1.2 and 3 and the points joined up in a curve – do the same on the other side and you now have your complete camber curve. Finally, carefully cut this curve out preserving the top part which is now your camber template.

All you now do is rest this template across the gunwales at any point along the length of the hull and you have the curve and camber height at that point – it will give you the shape of any beam at whatever point you position the curve along the length of the boat (Figure 101). The strongest and least wasteful way to make up a cambered deck beam is to laminate it – once the camber curve has been established for a particular beam, it can laminated in a number of ways. Here is just one method, where the curve is drawn down onto thick chipboard base and the curve is defined by a series of steel angle brackets bolted to the base so that their faces lie perpendicularly from the curve. Laminates can then be clamped to these steel with glue between them whilst the glue cures (Figure 102).

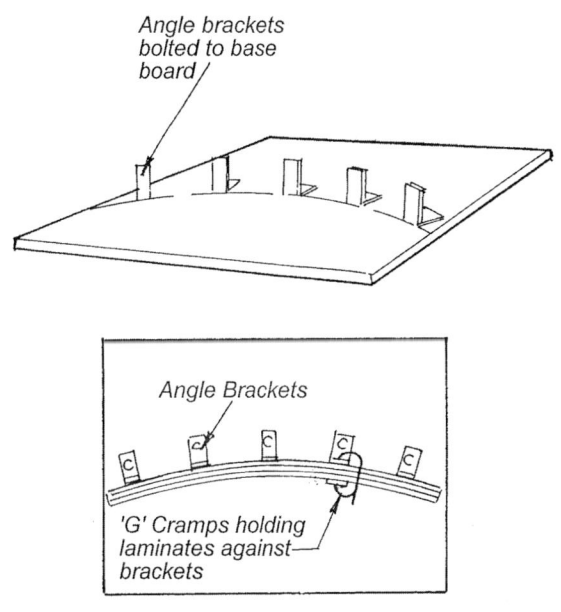

Fig 102. Laminating the deck beams.

If the brackets are a foot (0.3m) or so tall, several beams can be laminated at the same time as the curve remains the same for most of the beams – it is just the width that changes. Once the beams have been laminated, they can be removed from the jig and cleaned up ready to have their ends shaped to fit the join into the inwale (Figure 103).

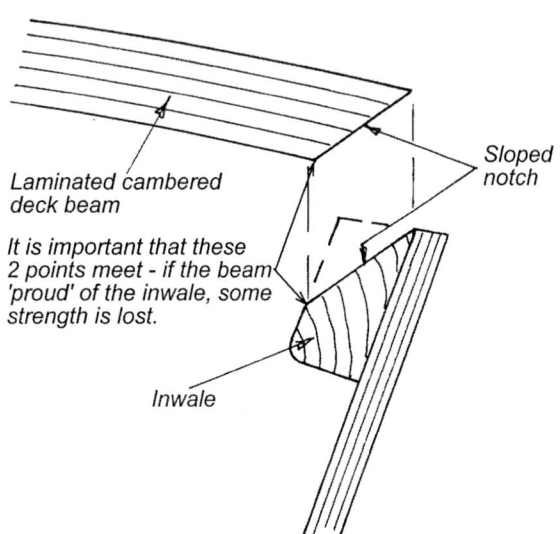

Fig 103. Housing the beams into the gunwale for cambered beams.

For both cambered and un-cambered decks, it is very important that the bottom of the cut and shaped end of the beams does not lie 'proud' of the inwale—this will mean that the beam is unable to use all it's stiffness and strength to support the deck. Sometimes the end of the beam is housed further into the inwale with a horizontal 'landing' cut onto the bottom of the notch cut into the inwale. However, this will weaken the inwale more than necessary, remember, it is always necessary to design the join so that we retain the structural integrity and stiffness of both items being joined.

An alternative way to make cambered beams is simply to cut them from the solid plank but if they are shaped on their underside, this gives them short grain areas which are weak (Figure 104).

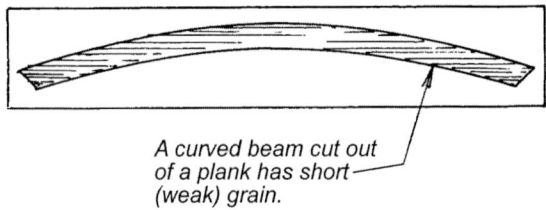

Fig 104. A weak cambered beam cut from a solid plank.

If the beam is up against a bulkhead then there is no reason why the bottom cannot be kept flat which avoids this problem and makes for an easily shaped beam (Figure 105).

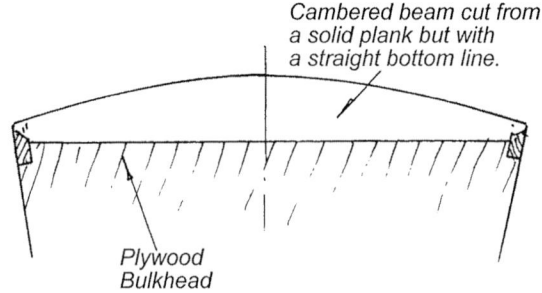

Fig 105. An easy way to fit a beam against a plywood frame/bulkhead—cut from solid plank with a flat bottom so that there is no short grain.

There will almost certainly not be a continuous beam across the aft end of the coachhouse because of the cockpit and companion entrance – but the beam camber template can be used here to gain the shape of the plywood bulkhead above the gunwale – the same can be done at any other intermediate bulkheads (Figure 106) – and these partial beams can be made up and fixed to the bulkheads.

Deck Structure

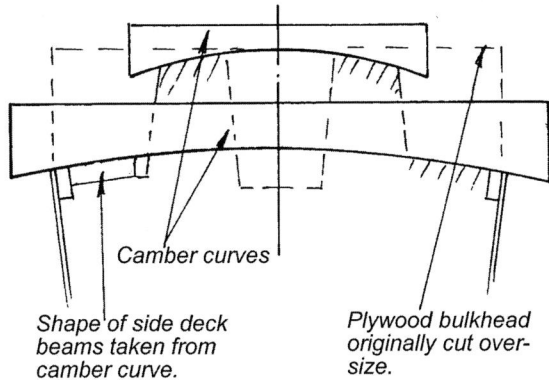

Fig 106. Marking the deck and cabin shape of the companion bulkhead.

If there are intermediate bulkheads running up under the side decks this makes it easier for establishing how the carlin runs and also for fixing it in place. If there are no intermediate bulkheads, the carlin needs to be fixed in position using simple plywood clamps – the width of the side deck at various points should be given on the drawings (Figure 107).

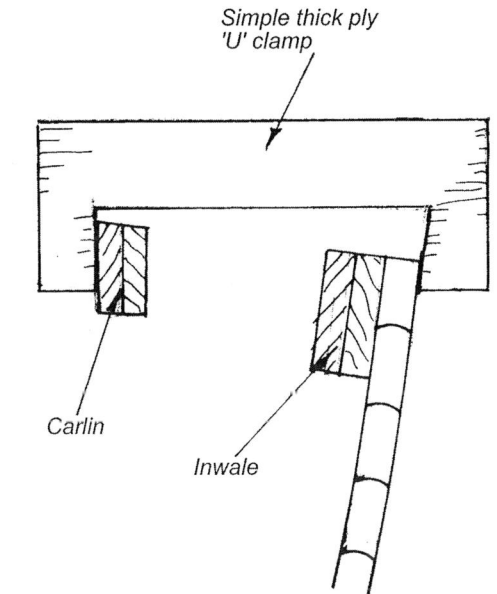

Fig 107. holding the deck carlin in place with a simple 'U' clamp.

The carlins can then be laminated either permanently in place or, so that they can be more easily cleaned up on the bench, dry fitted to the beams.

King planks and under deck blocking such as the breast hook can now be fitted and any specific blocks used for particular deck fittings can also be fitted in place. The whole deck structure should then be faired and cleaned up. You may want to do any final sanding and even varnishing/painting of the deck structure now, before the deck itself goes on – it is much easier at this stage, but do keep paints etc off the top surface of the deck structure where it will be glued to the decking.

8.1.2 The Cockpit

If you have not already done so, the cockpit should be fitted now. If there is an inboard engine, fit this first, but then make sure that it is well covered and protected and that all open ports in the engine are well blocked off to keep sawdust and debris out! Diesel tanks, fresh water tanks and possibly some plumbing may also be fitted at this stage. In fact some builders do much of the interior fit-out before the decking and coachhouse goes on – this is often a sensible way to work, but make sure that everything you do on the interior at this stage, is well protected.

You should always plan the cockpit so that major machinery can be removed through it, later, for maintenance – *do not build items in permanently, if you can avoid it!* An easy solution, assuming that the inboard engine is below the cockpit, is to make the whole cockpit sole removable by bedding it onto it's supporting structure and holding it down with bolts or screws in cup washers. Cockpit sole beams can be made removable in much the same way (Figure 108).

Fuel tanks are often tucked up out of the way under the side decks but if you can position these so that they can be removed too, so much the better.

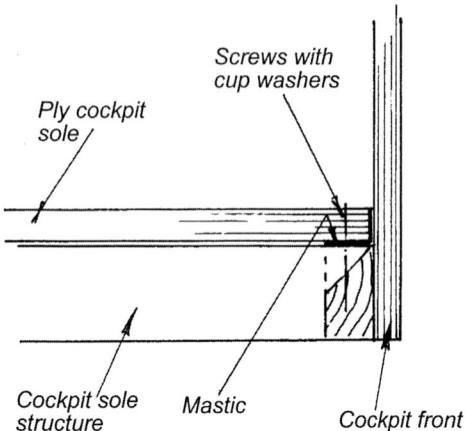

Fig 108. Removable cockpit sole.

8.1.3 The Deck

There is a question as to whether the deck or the coachhouse sides should be fitted next. There are certainly advantages to fitting the coachhouse sides from the point of view of easily fastening it to the carlin, but I prefer to fit the deck first just so that I do not damage the coachhouse sides when finishing the deck.

We will assume that the deck itself is plywood with perhaps, a layer of Teak decking on top. Solid laid Teak or Pitch Pine decks are fine and there are many older books that cover their construction but, as this is a book concerning larger plywood boats, it would seem ridiculous to ignore the fact that there are several advantages in at least having a plywood 'under deck'. A plywood deck acts as a massive strength member by imparting to the plan-form shape of the boat, stiffness and stability in shape. Rather than having individual planks running fore and aft, we have a sheet stiffener and strength member tying all parts of the deck together in the horizontal plane. Having spent many a sleepless night under a leaking laid deck, a plywood deck makes life dry!

The ply deck may go on in one thickness or in several thicknesses if there is a lot of camber – the rules and comments we used for the hull planking apply here. If the plywood is applied in several layers then joins in successive layers should be staggered – if not and only one thickness is applied, I like to use butt straps much like those for the hull planking. Of course, if there is blocking under the deck, these can act as butt straps too.

Some builders arrange joins in the plywood over the beams and stagger the joins – this is good practice so long as there is a large enough glue area to prevent movement (Figure 109).

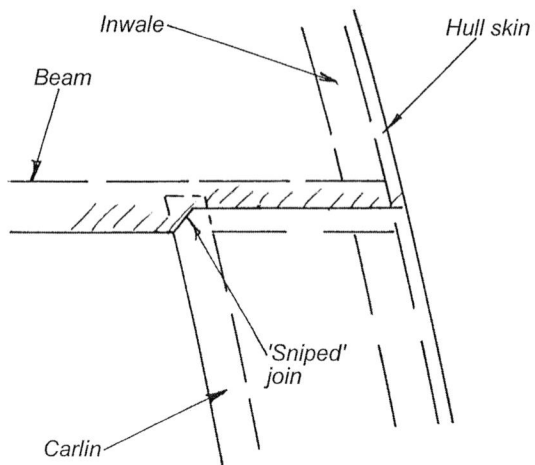

Fig 109. Plywood deck joins.

A typical layout for the plywood deck panels on a single thickness ply deck is shown in Figure 110.

Deck Structure

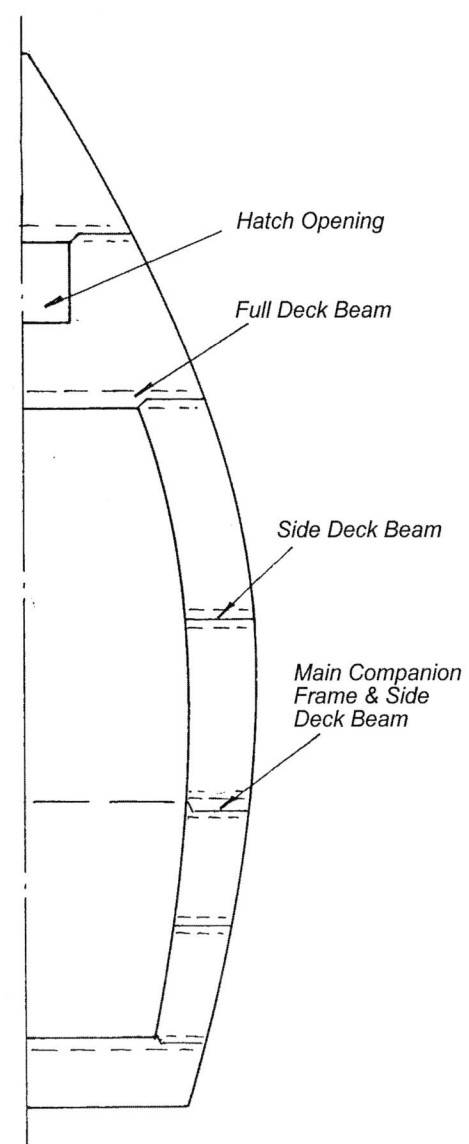

Fig 110. Layout of joins in deck plywood.

8.1.3.1 Sheathed Deck Covering

A simple plywood deck may be finished with a layer of course woven roving in epoxy resin. The same rules used for glass sheathing the hull, apply here except that you want to use a course weave cloth (300 gm or more) and leave the weave unfilled to give the deck some grip.

Do this sheathing before toerails etc are fitted and fit these items over the top of the sheathing (Figure 111).

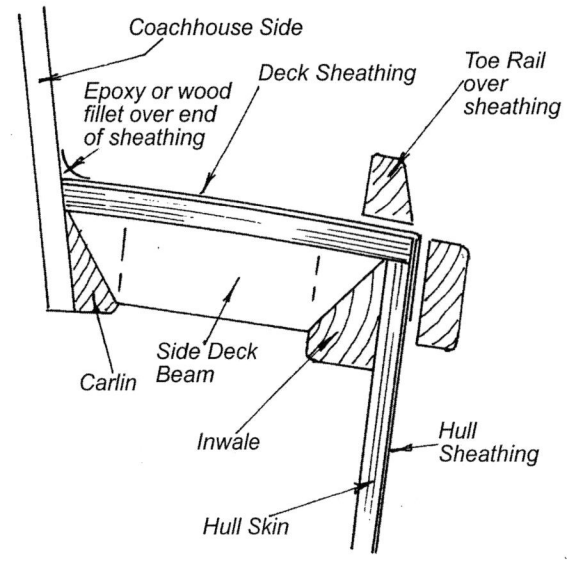

Fig 111. Sheathing the deck.

8.1.3.2 Teak Deck Covering

If you want a deck to be truly proud of, which shows off your craftsmanship, a plywood deck with Teak laid over it, is a good way to go. It is up to you how you want the Teak 'planks' to lie (Figure 112).

There is no need for the strips to be any thicker than 1/8" (3mm) or 3/16" (4mm) and 2" (50mm) wide is fine for most decks. Thicker teak is not necessarily a good idea as in contracting and expanding at a slightly different rate to the plywood under deck, the thicker strips may 'over-power' the epoxy glues used to stick them down.

Before the days of epoxy, the Yard I used to work for, would glue the Teak strips down using a Resorcinal glue and then fill the gaps between the Teak planks with a black butyl rubber compound. It was thought essential to make sure that the butyl rubber did not stick

Deck Structure

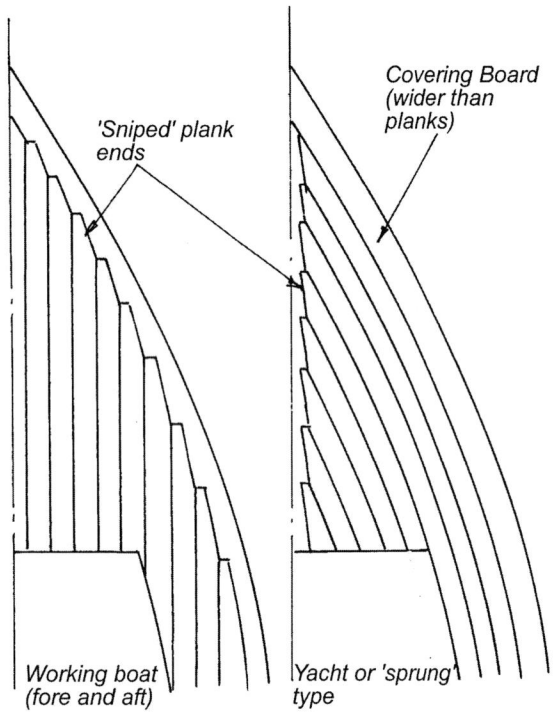

Fig 112. Two of the main ways of laying a Teak deck.

to the plywood surface at the bottom of the gap as this would cause problems with the differentials expansion between the Teak and plywood. To prevent adhesion to the bottom of the gap, cassette tape was laid down in the gap first.

With epoxies, the ideal way to lay the Teak is to glue it down with a thickened mix of epoxy with graphite added to it (often around 10% by volume) – this colours the mix black and the epoxy is allowed to squeeze between the planks and take on the roll of the black filler.

The procedure is to lay the planks out dry, cutting them to shape if possible. With planks that follow the mouth line (plan view curve of the gunwale), this is not always possible and so you simply have to glue and fasten individual planks and make up small quantities of the epoxy/graphite mix as you go. The planks are best fixed in place with ½" (12mm) long staples – use as few staples as possible and staple over old flex so that they can be more easily withdrawn after the epoxy has cured. Use small strips of 5mm thick aluminium to help maintain a 5mm gap between the planks.

Make sure the seams are all filled, allow the epoxy to cure fully and sand with a belt sander using 50 grit paper, finishing with 80 grit paper.

8.2 Coachhouses, Cabin Tops and Superstructures

You may find it helpful to 'mock' the coachhouse coaming and top up in hardboard so that you can check the shape and position of the ports (windows). In any case, a template will need to be taken of the coachhouse coaming (side) from the boat. Traditionally, the side of the coachhouse was often fitted outside a separate coaming to help make a water-tight join but now, with efficient glues, these 2 items are more often combined (Figure 113).

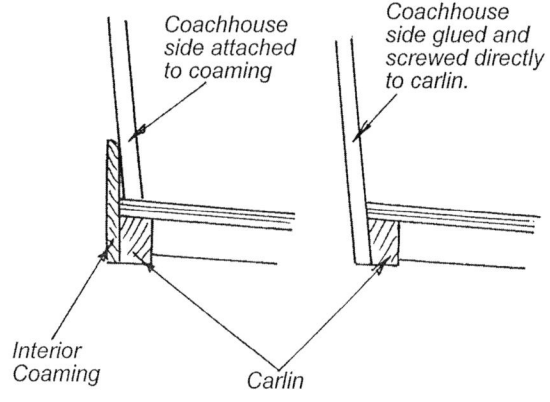

Fig 113. Traditional and modern methods of attaching the coachhouse sides.

There are several ways in which the coachhouse sides and top can be finished off and these are down on Figure 114.

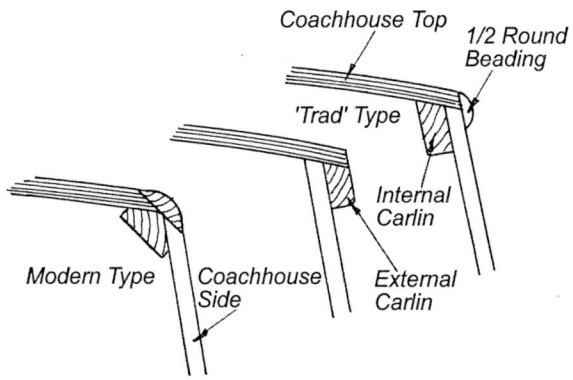

Fig 114. Different ways of joining the coachhouse sides and top.

Coachhouse sides may be plywood or solid wood (Mahogany was often used in the best yacht work) although using solid wood is very expensive in that you need to use wide and very high quality boards. Alternatively, you can strip plank the sides or, as in many American Catboats and Tugboats, use vertical wood staves which may be tongue and groove (Figure 115). Fairly thin tongue and groove staves can be used over and glued to a thin ply inner layer of plywood. The rounded fronts of Catboat cabins were often vertically staved.

Finishing and connecting the front to the sides of the coachhouse also have several different alternatives (Figure 116).

Cabin tops are often highly cambered and therefore have to be applied in 2 or 3 layers of thin plywood. If the top is of a highly 'compound' shape (with curves fore and aft and athwartship), the layers of plywood may need to be put on in diagonal strips around 5" (125mm) wide. The whole top can be finished off with a glass sheathing. If the top is applied using this diagonal method, it is

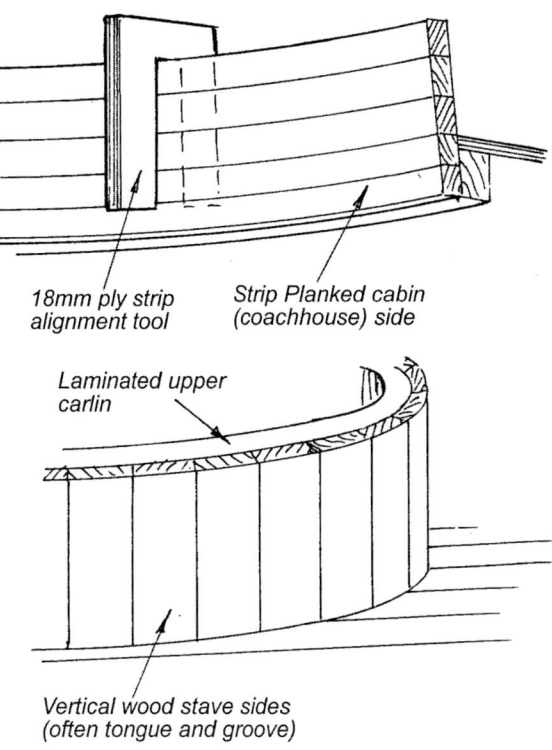

Fig 115. Strip planked and vertically staved coachhouse sides.

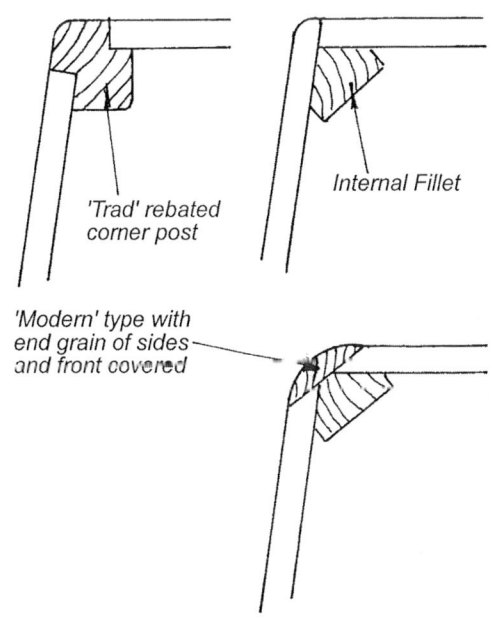

Fig 116. Different ways of connecting the coachhouse sides and front.

Deck Structure

quite likely that fore and aft stringers will need to be fitted first, in order to give enough support to the thin diagonal plywood planking (Figure 117). The actual plywood top is, when fully glued, very stiff and strong—therefore, if you need to save weight or require a few inches more headroom it is often possible to remove many of the supporting beam and stringers after the top is finished. The easiest way to do this, is to consider the beams etc as temporary during construction and fit them to the coachhouse carlin temporarily. The top would be laminated in situ but not glued to the supporting structure. The top is then removed, those beams and stringers that can be taken out, removed and the top glued and fastened back in place.

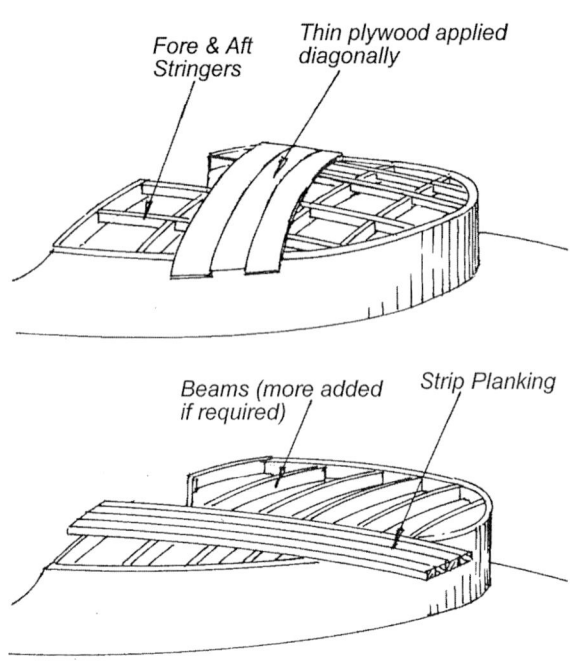

Fig 117—above. Diagonally planked and strip planked coachhouse tops.

Coachhouse tops may also be strip planked. Fore and aft stringers are not required but maybe, more temporary beams/moulds are.

The strip planked top may be treated in the same way as the diagonally planked top and be removed, so that some beams can be taken out of the structure and also so that the underside of the top may be sheathed in glass. This makes a very stiff and strong shell top (Figure 117).

If the coachhouse top is applied in one thickness, the layout of the joins is much the same as used for the main deck with joins made over beams. If it is put on in two or more thicknesses, stagger the joins.

Above and below, two views of Aquiles Rosner's Kari 3 showing the fit-out of the cockpit and cabin top. The cabin top is plywood but much of the cockpit is solid wood.

Chapter 9
THE CARE & REPAIR
OF STRIP PLANKED HULLS

Normally, care for a glass sheathed Cedar hull is much the same as for a sheathed ply or wood hull in that any breach of the sheathing should be immediately seen to. A glass sheathed Cedar hull is very tough especially when the sheathing has been applied with epoxies and normal scrapes and bashes will not cause any problems even cosmetically. However, Cedar will absorb water faster than hardwood planking and this will cause further damage to the bond between the Cedar and the glass sheathing and therefore, any breach through the sheathing must be repaired promptly.

Repair to the glass sheathing is simply a matter of cutting and grinding back the glass until solid material is found. The glass which has come adrift from the hull will be white in colour and this should be cut away. When all loose material has been removed, the edge of the remaining glass sheathing surrounding the damaged area should be ground to a shallow angle. Allow the wood to dry out thoroughly and then carry out any repairs necessary. A glass patch can now be applied using fabric and resin to match the original overlapping the ground area. Once this has cured, it can be ground to match in with the original material.

Canoes often sustain small but deep scratches in the sheathing. In this case sand carefully with some 80 grit sandpaper without going right through to the wood and feather the sanding out from the scratch over a distance of around 1 1/2" (36mm) all round. Mask off the area outside this and lay in a piece of glass cloth. You can lay a piece of PVC or waxed paper over the resin and cloth and use a sqeegee to remove air and excess resin. Once the resin has cured, peel off the PVC and sand/polish the edges. If damage has been sustained to the wood, sand through and fill the wood with epoxy/wood fibre before repeating the above.

Sometimes, after a bad impact, the sheathing may be intact but the wood below it may be shattered. On a canoe, this can be tested by pressing the hull. If it gives or feels spongy, then the wood is likely to have been cracked. In this case, simply drill a small hole through the sheathing on the high side and inject warm resin so that it seeps into all the shattered wood fibre. Use a hair drier to help cure the resin. If the glass sheathing has been damaged as well, remove it as before and open out the damaged planking fibres. Soak resin into them and push back and hold in place with tape. Finish the repair as already described.

On larger boats, and if several planks have been damaged on a canoe, then a more extensive repair is necessary. First, remove the damaged wood so that there is only sound wood left. It is better to cut out a hole which is not square or rectangular but is a more irregular shape. This will give a stronger repair and will be less obvious. There are now 2 ways of proceeding. You can cover the area of the hole with PVC and plank up a hull piece over size, over the hole. This will then be close to the correct curvature and it can then be marked from the inside, removed and then trimmed to fit the hole exactly. The planks should be laid up to match the hull planking. The second method, is to plank directly into the hole. This is usually the way to do it, if the damaged area is quite extensive and runs fore and aft for several feet or a couple of metres. If the hull has no frames, then temporary moulds will need to be made up and attached to the inside of the hull to give a shape to work against. Again, match up the planks and scarf them together on the hull in a well staggered manner. On a large repair, the glass sheathing should be cut well back so that the new sheathing extends well away from the patch.

Where there is framing and the repairs are required to the framing as well, this is usually done before the planking is repaired in order to retain the correct hull shape. The whole operation will be made more difficult if the planking has been nailed together, in which case there will be much frustration in removing the damaged planking and nails. If you are using epoxies however, the new planking can go back with few nails.

Above—a 21' Skua by Toni Reiter showing off her varnished planking and ready for a sail!